The STARSEED DIALOGUES

The
STARSEED
DIALOGUES

Soul Searching
the Universe

PATRICIA CORI

North Atlantic Books
Berkeley, California

Published by
North Atlantic Books
P.O. Box 12327
Berkeley, California 94712

Cover photograph by Alberto Fanelli
Cover design by Brad Greene
Book design by Brad Greene

Printed in the United States of America

The Starseed Dialogues: Soul Searching the Universe is sponsored by the Society for the Study of Native Arts and Sciences, a nonprofit educational corporation whose goals are to develop an educational and cross-cultural perspective linking various scientific, social, and artistic fields; to nurture a holistic view of arts, sciences, humanities, and healing; and to publish and distribute literature on the relationship of mind, body, and nature.

North Atlantic Books' publications are available through most bookstores. For further information, call 800-733-3000 or visit our website at www.northatlanticbooks.com.

Library of Congress Cataloging-in-Publication Data

Cori, Patricia.
   The starseed dialogues : soul searching the universe / Patricia Cori.
       p. cm.
   ISBN 978-1-55643-783-0
   1. Sirius—Miscellanea. 2. Mayas—Prophecies. 3. Prophecies (Occultism)
4. Esoteric astrology. 5. Civilization, Modern—21st century—Forecasting.
I. Title.
   BF1724.4.S57C67 2008
   133.9—dc22

2008047890

1 2 3 4 5 6 7 8 9 UNITED 14 13 12 11 10 09

*This work is dedicated
to the Family of Light,
those whom I have been honored to meet along the way,
those who have shared the magic with me,
those who have shared their questions
to be brought to the Council,
and everyone,
near and far,
who seeks to make ours
a more beautiful world.*

Acknowledgments

I would like to acknowledge friends and associates who have helped in the rebirthing of this book. To Robert Phoenix, whose determination to share the works with a greater public opened doors—my love around you. Very special thanks to Richard Grossinger, my publisher, who believed in the Sirian teachings and has given me so much support and freedom to share their truth. I am deeply grateful to Hisae Matsuda, my dedicated project editor, who has guided this book and the trilogy through their metamorphosis to their new polished versions. Special thanks too to Adrienne Armstrong, for her excellent editing, always holding true to the voice of the Council. To all the people at North Atlantic Books: Brad Greene for his powerful graphics, Drew Cavanaugh, Sarah Serafimidis, my publicist Allegra Harris, and everyone else working behind the scenes—your professionalism and love shines through every step of the book's journey.

Many special people in my life have supported me throughout this process of discovery: Franco, my soulmate, never falters. His patience and steadfast support have been the foundation of home, from where I have been able to fly to other realms and always return. So many friends, old and new, who have encouraged and celebrated the journey: Damien, Laura, Beata, Andrea, Kalli, Judith, Claudia, Omnia, Manar, ... the list is endless. To Acharika, a very special lady, thanks for your generosity and understanding of what really matters. And always, to my mother, Sara, who hovers from the other side, sending angels to guide the way.

The Circles of Light around the world, lightworkers who join with me in my seminars and soulquest journeys, thank you too— for your trust, your sense of truth and humility, and your celebration of the Sirian wisdom. We are shining the light out around this great planet, connecting the dots.

Table of Contents

Preface

Here we are—spinning wildly in the whir of our changing reality—and everywhere our opportunities to co-create reality beckon to be brought to manifestation.

No doubt, there is untold chaos in our world—we are all too familiar with the rattling of sabers and the violence wars. Yet, as we gaze upon the horizon of human expression, we observe an incredible landscape of awakening souls, rising from the opium fields and standing for beauty, truth, and the loving way.

The brilliance of the human spirit shines everywhere around us—through the shadows, through the dust, through the darkness itself. It is simply a breathtaking thing to behold. Do you see what I see?

My life work as a healer and dedicated scribe to the Speakers of the Sirian High Council has brought me to the far corners of our glorious Planet Earth, assimilating the Earth Codes and learning the mysteries of the ancients—barely scratching the surface of the deep fabric of our history and the mysteries of the Universe.

Everywhere I have found the vestiges of the struggle of darkness and light, where man and deity have written the course of humankind upon the sands of time. We have triumphed—we have survived. We have been born again, born anew. We have risen from the ashes, just as we are rising now—soaring above the clouds ... knowing ... sure ... God (however perceived) IS.

"There is order in chaos," say the Speakers. The divine imprint is laced throughout the most inconsonant layers of reality, just as the light of Spirit penetrates even the darkest corners of the Cosmos of Soul.

Now is a time to shake off all residual fear and the doubt that has been strewn in our path, inebriating many who have lost the way. It is a time to stand in our truth, perhaps as we never have before, and to call upon all others to stand in theirs, so that together we can raise the consciousness of the group soul—bringing healing, bringing forgiveness, bringing illumination to the living of our world.

We are the caretakers of Gaia, each with an assignment—each with a key. It is our unity and voice that will bring our Earth back to Center, where the pendulum no longer swings its fury back and forth, holding us in the duality.

We have a mission. We have a calling. Let us raise the flame!

Our mutating consciousness is crystallizing within us, at the cellular level, as our complex DNA filaments reweave the light-coded strands of extra-dimensional intelligence. We are in the light, we are the light ... moving rapidly towards the New Dawn of civilization.

Where there is light, there is nothing to fear.

Only the wonder of a not-so-distant horizon, where harmony has been restored, is the reality ... and it is there that we are headed.

Be at peace—fully conscious, contributing what you can to the human experience and breathing life back into Gaia.

Ours is a beautiful world.

Seek love, light, and the greatness of humanity and you will find the beauty everywhere around you.

I, for one, will not be dragged into the valley of despair and powerlessness.

Will you join me?

Let us stand tall upon the mountaintops,

blowing the dark clouds away.

—*Patricia Cori*

1

The Sirius–Ra Connection

Of the three brilliant stars of the Sirius system, only one remains in the physical realm, as you understand it from the three-dimensional perspective. This celestial fire is referred to in your scientific communities as "Sirius A." We Sirians know it as the deity, Sothis, and so it has been recognized by the ancient Egyptians, who knew so much about our civilizations and their own starseed linkage to us.

Located in that quadrant of the Universe that you identify as the "Canis Major" constellation, Sothis can, in a cosmic sense, be considered directly "upstream" from your solar system, referring to its relative position in the Milky Way galaxy. A highly charged stellar field, it rains its high-end electromagnetic currents over the body of Ra (your solar system), affecting the solar activity and planetary response of all that comprises your solar family.

We, who sit on the Sirian High Council, are light body beings who have actively experienced the ascension of the sister Sirian Star, Satais, recognized only recently by your scientists as a "dwarf" star and named "Sirius B." We have imagined the unimaginable, known the unknowable ... and passed from the density into the light.

That monumental celestial event—the passing of Satais through the astral cord, linking her physical expression to her higher soul vibration—sent waves of unfathomable energies coursing through those three-dimensional fields where she had held resonance, until that glorious moment of her passage out of the universe of matter.

Casting off the physical body, Satais sent untold quantities of her denser gases (elements heavier than hydrogen) racing through what you call the "Milky Way" galaxy, as her entire system shed its physical cloak and moved to a new station in the higher realms of conscious awareness.

Your Solar Deity, Ra, directly downstream, was enormously affected, as were the neighboring stellar bodies that form the galaxy of stars in their complexity: all that they emit, exchange, and receive in the flow of consciousness that defines the cosmic sea.

This interstellar energy exchange is one of the fundamental aspects of the Sirius–Ra connection. It is the celestial background for our conscious involvement with the sentient beings of your solar system.

There is so much conflicting information surrounding the question of the interaction of Sirius with events unfolding on our planet. A lot of people speak of the "Planet" Sirius, rather than the star or star system; others refer to Sirians not as "light beings" but as "dark warriors"—warning of their interference in earth affairs.

Can you shed more light upon the dynamics and configuration of the Sirian star system and the current role of Sirius in earth affairs?

Ours is a complex stellar family: a multidimensional trinity of parallel universes in which our three stars currently hold resonance. As such, the Sirian Sisterhood "imprints" the Cosmos with the vibratory signature of a nonlinear fractal design, perpetually co-creating the multidimensional Universe in a breathtaking array of stellar and planetary harmonics and cosmometric proportions.

You can understand why we are so attuned to the concept of triangulation, the dynamic interrelationships of aspects that form the numerical imprint of three ... and why it is so very basic to the knowledge we attempt to share with you as we communicate through our instrument, the channel who brings our message to you.

It is the combined consciousness of our three stellar deities that defines the One and, as such, the evolutionary progression of each is defined by the All—the Sisterhood of Three.

If we may use the metaphor of the combined notes of a symphony, the three sister stars would be best described as a musical chord of three harmonious notes on the diatonic scale, but each sounding from a different octave.

We ask you to imagine how each is a reflection of the other and how the stellar framework forms a multidimensional merkaba of light, sound, and soul. That music rings eternal through the dimensions, uniting all the consciousness units of this celestial sphere—a bass chord in the music of infinity.

Together as One (for we are One, despite our differences), all conscious beings of the realm form the chorus, creating our overlying melody, as the orchestra plays the song of Creation under the superb direction of Prime Creator ... the Grand Maestro.

Can you tell us whether or not there are planets currently orbiting Sirius and if so, are there three-dimensional beings from any even-

*tual Sirius A planets involved in human evolution? I am eager to
know if there are planets still orbiting the ascended stars as well.*

Let us elaborate your first question regarding the stellar composition of Sirius and the planets of each stellar deity, with the
specifics of each:

Sothis (Sirius A) shines in your three-dimensional holographic
galaxy as the brightest light in your northern hemisphere—far
more luminous than your own star, Ra, and the fifth closest star
(in linear terms) to yours.

It currently holds vibration on the third dimension, gracing
your celestial canopy with the brilliant light that has long inspired
civilizations of *Homo sapiens,* since the time of your inception, as
it has others—on the sister planets of your solar system—com-
prising the physical, spiritual, and mental bodies of Ra.

It was once the gravitational anchor of a number of planetary
bodies similar to your Earth, upon which liquid water was available in abundance to all life forms and climates were warm and
steamy—much like those of your equatorial zones.

Extremely dense atmospheres shielded the inner planets of
Sothis from the scorching ultraviolet rays and gases, allowing
untold species of aquatic life as well as incredibly complex fauna
to flourish on those planetary surfaces: from the minutiae of single cell amoebae, to the complexity of the most exquisite verte-
brates—many of which exist on Earth as well.

Countless species mirroring biological earth life (those with
which you are familiar and endless others, still unidentified) exist

on other planets, particularly within the family of planetary bodies that comprise your own solar system.

The organization of subatomic particles always follows the intelligent design of Creation and these cosmometric patterns appear throughout all time, space, and dimension.

Many are the creatures of your oceans—from the deep, dark abyss of the deepest seas to sun-laced shallow waters—that also procreate in the vast oceans across the Cosmos of Soul.

Although you have studied and observed countless species of your oceans, your marine biologists have yet to understand, in its entirety, the complexity of form and interdependency within the seas. They have not yet understood the interplay between the layers of light and dark, treble and bass, absorption and refraction and the weaving of consciousness from sea floor to surface and back again.

Certain species of the seas are so remote in your most inaccessible environments that you have yet to even imagine their existence—and yet they are there, as they are elsewhere, in the Cosmos.

As close as your deepest oceans, then, life exists where you have been taught to believe it cannot—as it does not fit into the boundaries of what science has allowed (until now) as "probable environments" in which biological life can flourish.

Despite the various belief systems, speculation, and hypotheses of your more conservative scientific voices, we assure you that life (as it occurs on Earth) abounds, in varied and similar forms, at several stopping points in your solar realm ... and beyond.

Life is the driving force of the universe of matter. It is the essential nature of the Universe! All is thought; all is motion; all is manifestation. Earth, which in many ways you still perceive as the center of your universe, is but a drop in the greatest ocean— a second in the infinity of timeless beauty.

As for Sirius A, our three-dimensional star: we do confirm to you that, at this point on the space-time continuum, there is no intelligent (as you understand it) biological life in its greater stellar body.

What you are being told about intelligent beings from Sirius A somehow "invading your space" is not representative of any Sirian reality with which we are familiar.

What does exist there is more easily described as the "subatomic data base" of previous biological life forms—awaiting the proper coordinates on that time line to reactivate.

Therefore, in answer to your question and with an emphatic collective voice from the Sirian High Council, we reiterate that, currently, there are no sentient species from this realm, the three-dimensional aspect of the Trinity of Sirius, in any way interfering with human affairs or earth biology.

Satais (Sirius B) was once the giant of the triangulation of stars that comprise the Sirian family of solar deities. Throughout its duration in the 3D realm, it was the leviathan of the solar trinity as it was the life-bearer of twelve planetary satellites that have all ascended to the higher dimensions.

It currently holds frequency on the sixth dimension, and the light bodies of those planets that orbited Satais continue to hold the celestial coordinates—the harmonics—which reflect the dynamic makeup of that system.

Not all ascended Sirians reside here with us in the sixth dimension, but we, Sirians of the High Council, come to you from this light frequency. Some have gone on to higher realms; some have retrograded to lower densities to work with other life forms, focusing consciousness to reach attunement there—in very much the same way as we reach you, via our dedicated instrument, Trydjya.

What is seen orbiting Sothis in your three-dimensional telescopic fields is the skeletal form of that stellar being, left behind as a marker of what once was a part of your density. It ascended long ago into light body, as have the planets and living beings that resided there.

Of the many beings who have progressed with Satais, it is those of us in this dimension (the sixth) who are directly concerned with earth affairs, for reasons that have been amply explained to you in prior works ... but we wish to reemphasize that there are other light beings from the Satais imprint, who are bringing their love and wisdom to the many other worlds in need of assistance, at this phase of Ra's imminent ascension.

They are heart-centered, loving participants in the spiral stream upon which we all contribute enormous energy and experience, as it is the mission of all light beings to assist others, further down the spiral, in their journey back to Source.

You have this to look forward to in ways you may still find difficult to imagine ... perhaps not until you reach the next level of awareness, when you are truly living in unconditional love for all the people, places, beings, and life forms—loving even the darkest ones, whom you know will eventually return to Source, just like you.

Anu (Sirius C) is the third of our complex stellar interface. In the three-dimensional phase of its development, it was the source of life for five primary planetary bodies and a significant quantity of lifeless (in biological terms) formations, which most closely resemble that which you have identified as the "asteroid" in your own system.

It passed to the fourth dimension and still resonates to the consciousness of that density, determined by the evolutionary progress of that Solar Logos and the celestial deities of her physical being.

As you have gleaned from our texts, *The Sirian Revelations,* Nebiru was one planet of Anu that has remained in the 3D realm. Of the intelligent life forms of the other four, there have been species that have retrograded into the earth biosphere (at different points in your planet's evolution) to assist and serve the human race.

Amongst these were the predecessors of the Dolphin Beings— made immortal through the teachings of the Ancient Dogon peoples of the land mass you know as Africa.

So, just to clarify this point: you are telling us that by "multidimensional stellar trinity" you mean that Sirius A exists on the third dimension, Sirius B is on the sixth, and Sirius C still remains on the fourth dimension?

That is correct. Because Sirius is a composite three-star deity, existing, simultaneously, on three different dimensional levels (third, fourth, and sixth), it serves as a multidimensional portal— a sort of Gatekeeper of the universe of matter.

Many Ascended Masters pass through this portal, moving in and out of the third dimension at will, as did the Christed One.

As to your second question concerning the orbits of ascended planets, please consider that your perception of orbital patterns is a three-dimensional perspective of what is actually a multidimensional experience of celestial interactions. In the higher dimensions, one perceives the energy flows between conscious beings: from the most unfathomably minute bacteria to entire super galaxies. From this point of view, you will be able to imagine how planets still reverberate and interact with their mother stars, regardless of their celestial movements.

You are learning, dear one, about the music of Creation.

It is about resonance, harmony, and light.

It is so difficult to conceive of this multidimensional dynamic described in your last answer and it defies all the scientific information available to us.

Yes, it is naturally difficult for you to conceive of the higher dimensions from the physical plane. We do understand how, when you attempt to tread these uncharted roads, you can feel you are lost or losing your way ... in every sense. After all, the straight and narrow roads of convention are by far more clearly marked and so much "safer" than traveling new and adventurous pathways.

No doubt it is problematical for you, attempting to share such concepts with those around you, for, as a member of the awakening, you are likely to be surrounded by those who are still deep in sleep. They will consider you just as much a radical as the "daring" were back in the Dark Ages of human history.

They will still consider any far-reaching thoughts a "danger" to the status quo to which they cling for safety, in these hours of untold change and revolution in earthly affairs.

During those days of humanity's absolute ignorance of the mechanical universe, merely suggesting that your world was not a flat surface from which ships would fall into the abyss if they ventured too far from shore was considered heresy ... punishable by imprisonment or even death.

Imagine what such courts would have done to anyone of you—with the wealth of information currently available to your contemporary scientists and, moreover, with the daring and bold revelations that you are now claiming as "new visions" on the meaning of life in the heavens.

We welcome you to the realm of free thinkers. The information is available to you—but only you can decide whether you are ready and willing to stretch yourself to consider what lies beyond the established theories of conformity.

Always remember that what pushes science and all scientific assumption forward is the desire of the awakening to challenge the dogma of established belief systems and to explore new pathways upon the roads of discovery: the quest of all conscious beings to understand the Universe and the role each of us is to play within it.

All grow when the stagnation of dogmatic presumptions (for your scientific body of information is based on presumptions of how what lies beyond your world is actually formed) is replaced with newly acquired knowledge and insights. All eventually see how such expanded visions shed light upon the collective experience of life in the Cosmos of Soul.

What is needed by those paradigm busters who defy and question authority are unbridled courage and a clear intellect to challenge, review, rethink, and eventually change the way they and others perceive the infinite layers of reality.

Forgive me if this is a foolish question—but I am curious as to why you refer to our star, Ra, as male ... but to the Sirian stars as female. As a feminist I find this offensive and I would like to know why you make this distinction?

Our use of your male/female nomenclature and identification is not at all gender-inspired. Rather, it is simply a question of receptivity and the nature of energy exchanging within the polar limitations of the lower dimensions.

As Ra is a solitary star, it is of a nature that is far more yang-like in its focus and self-awareness and you must understand that we speak not only of your Sun's relationship to the planets, but his interrelationships with the solar deities of the entire galaxy of stars ... and yes, with those of other dimensions as well.

Sirius, with its interrelatedness and tri-fold aspects, is a far more receptive stellar environment—more of a yin-like vibrational field.

In our realms, there is no female/male distinction—no superiority of gender. There is only the complement of one to the other, for we have long ago learned that both are equal and complementary aspects of the One and there is everything to celebrate in the perfection of the electromagnetic harmonies—the yin/yang vibration.

Neither exists without the other in the greater Universe in which you, dear one, are recognized as pure vibrational essence—rather than your gender, color, age, or any other physical attributes!

Is there conscious communication between the stars of Sirius, despite the fact that they exist on different layers?

If you intend this question to mean "conscious communication" between and amongst the stellar beings themselves, yes, there most definitely exists a flow of consciousness, energy transference, and continuous dialogue between them. They are interactive and energetically co-creative in every sense.

There are incredible streams of energy flowing between them, between the dimensions—affecting each, affecting all.

They are known throughout the Greater Galaxy as *The Sisterhood.*

As for the exchange of consciousness between individual units of living beings in these star systems, let us say that we hold the awareness, the memory, and the codes to link to sentient beings on other layers at will, which is determined by the attainment of the resonant frequencies.

Are there planets currently bearing any activated life forms at all orbiting Sothis?

There no longer exist planets bearing complex biological life forms within the system of Sothis, due to the cosmic events that have redefined this complex stellar environment. Essentially, these have created:

* Heat too extreme for atmospheres to form.
* Enormous magnetic interference by the shell of Satais in its fifty-year orbit of Sothis, causing an unfathomable electrical charge, which prevents the development of any and all electromagnetic bio-forms.
* Extreme radiation pouring into the star system from the skeletal form of Satais, which destroys biological configurations at the subcellular level.

However, we ask you always to remember that intelligence exists throughout the Cosmos—it is the design, the mathematical perfection of all things. It is the cosmometry of every particle of dust; every atom; every element; the substance and the wave.

If you take the leap from your understanding of life as being "biological" in nature, to an expanded awareness of consciousness in nonbiological forms, you will understand the infinite splendor of life in the Cosmos of Soul. Then, yes—you will understand more succinctly what we intend when we state that life does exist in the stellar body of Sothis.

I want to be sure I really understand your meaning here. Are you inferring that there is an unknown life form in these realms?

We are speaking not of an unknown form of life but of one that may not conform to your earthly definitions of what would constitute a "living being."

Life (as we intend units of conscious subatomic particles, intent upon creating form when the proper coordinates and alignments are reached) fills the body of Sothis, the Sirian deity that shines brightest in your canopy of stars ... at the ultraviolet frequency.

Nothing is dead in the Universe. All is consciousness creating, forming, being ... transforming and beginning again and again.

With regard to the Nebiruans, whom you have identified as the problematic three-dimensional race of aliens trapped in an elliptical orbit between Sirius and Ra, there is significant disinformation and confusion circulating among even the most informed people in our circles of light. There are sources here who declare that these are actually intelligent light beings who have ascended to the higher dimensions after assisting our ancestors, the Atlanteans, and who are serving us, as you claim to be, from the higher realms.

Please help us to understand how we are to rectify this discrepancy with what you state regarding this civilization and their intended involvement in earth affairs.

The Nebiruan population remains entrapped in the lowest forms of survival consciousness in the inner world of that planet, which continues its elliptical orbit from Sothis (Sirius A) to Ra (your Sun), very much a part of the three-dimensional spatial reality— as is Gaia (Earth).

Descendants from this ancient population have also interbred with *Homo sapiens* in earth gravity and they have stolen the power, positioning themselves as the self-imposed, elite rulers of your planet—hence your troublesome connection to them.

From the hour of late Atlantis, they used their influence upon the Dark Priesthood to create the kind of technologies that haunt you again today: electromagnetic stimulation of the lower energy centers; mind-control technologies; the acceleration of ego-centered consciousness and separation, in order to push your race into ideological separation and obedience.

In that era of intervention in Atlantean affairs, they altered the values and perceptions of the ancient civilization by building upon the people's primordial fear of survival, creating conflict and wars, and by introducing sacrificial rites, mass control methodologies, and mind manipulation into the culture.

These, the darkest acts of forced submission, involved violent and public death for those whose misfortune it was to be targeted by the Dark Priesthood, who operated under the hypnotic commands of their Annunaki lords. With the flow of human blood into communal temple grounds, the life force of the Atlanteans— their collective will—was drawn from them, while those sacred sites suffocated under the weight of human despair.

We do not acknowledge Nebiruans as having ascended to higher realms. Of the ascended extraterrestrials, there are teams of lightworkers from other dimensions now working with the Nebiruans (just as we are assisting you), attempting to guide them back to the light and to provide assistance for them in their passage out of the darkness—both physically and spiritually.

You need to know that this is the way of multidimensional consciousness. We take our giant steps and then reach out to those who have fallen behind, lost in the shadowy vapors that can veil the path of soul progression.

In the magnificence of love unfolding, no one is alone.

No one is forsaken.

No one is abandoned.

That is the state of our eternal existence.

As for the discrepancy and confusion surrounding this and other questions brought forward by those who speak to you of galactic sociology, know that inevitably it is that which brings the heart to celebration that you will know as Truth and so we cannot spell it out for you in irrefutable terminologies.

It is for you to discern what rings as Truth there in your heart. Only within the center of your being can Truth be found and that is a search you must take on for yourselves, as dedicated seekers upon the spiral that leads you to the bright light.

All information presented to you is potentially formed of the opinion, interpretation, and (most significantly) the intention of the one who brings it forth for you as the final word.

We bring you Truth, through the channel, **as we know it:** as we know if from our long and luminous journey into the sixth dimension. Unquestionably, as we move further along the magnificent spiral, what we hold as Truth today may very well transmute into new understandings and higher awareness tomorrow. This is the majesty of our journey, as it is yours ... as it is that of every conscious being in the Cosmos.

It is the awe and wonder of the entire process of soul climbing higher.

Indeed, it is the reason we exist: to climb to the mountaintops, to seek the light of Truth, to learn the purpose of our journey and our mission and above all, to celebrate the magnificence of all we discover, serving the All along the way.

How do you experience your opening to us as we open to you? Can you feel your love for me as viscerally as I feel my love for you? I know that contact is happening in these moments. It's here; it's now.

Beautiful starseed child, we do so feel your love pouring through us. It is the love emanating from the human heart that draws us to you and into your realm and it is as clear and bright as the most perfect crystal in its purity of intent and emotion.

We are capable of attuning to you and reaching resonance when you are in center—in heart consciousness. That connection is the music and the light that pours through the dimensions—knowing no limitation or division. The sweetness of that melody strums within us the strings of compassion and tenderness that are so delightfully human-like, so utterly compelling, in their emotional expression.

We cannot describe such experience as being "visceral" to us; rather, it is the unbridled joy of unconditional love and the knowing that all is perfection in the vastness of All That Is.

So when you feel us feeling you, in love, what is the story that you glean from the experience?

There is no "story" to love permeating the dimensions—no history nor time nor place of the immensity that is Love. There is only light: only beauty and the expansion of the All.

The higher we climb upon the Great Spiral of return to Source, the brighter the light of Source ... and we remember.

We remember the purpose and the music and the dance.

We feel your love: it moves through us, echoes of song, ripples of light. You feel ours as well. We feel you feeling it, feeling us, being One.

When you gather in your circles of light, we feel the love permeating all space, all time.

When you embrace a child, speak to the animals, celebrate a soft breeze as it brushes gently upon your cheek, we feel your love shimmering golden upon the cosmic wind, across the no-time.

When you fight for a better world, when you cry out in sorrow, when you reach the heights of the human experience, fighting injustice, searching for Truth—there, too, are we feeling you: feeling your love and pain, for both are mirrors of the heart. Both mirror the immensity of human emotion.

The intellect may question beauty, but the heart embraces it—unconditionally.

Love is all there is.

How can you say all is beauty and light when before us we see such degradation, destruction, and death? Many of us feel that humanity is in its darkest hour and there is no light at the end of this tunnel. How can you expect us to embrace the idea that, in a violent world such as ours, all is Love?

There is no challenge in finding beauty in light, where all is filled with the glow and wonder of Spirit. Souls in perennial evolution, the test we have placed before our own eyes is to find beauty even in darkness, for that is our learning field. There is where we learn the responsibility of our own creations and is that not our true purpose—our reason to exist?

These are the tests of the true Initiate.

We accept the darkness (insofar as we learn to own our responsibility for our part in it) and we strive to shine the light of consciousness into those dark corners. We are grateful to know how majestically we finally move beyond it—an experience that you, the awakening, are soon to share.

We do not have expectations of what you are to believe or embrace as Truth, for we have always told you that it resides in your hearts. However, sweet soul, we do invite you to rise above your despair to:

Seek light and you will feel it shine upon you.

Seek love and you will feel its embrace.

Seek forgiveness and you will quickly learn the purpose of the shadow.

We are so grateful to you for what you bring to the human race. How blessed we are to have you shining your light upon us! May we have the pleasure of knowing more about you—who sits on the Sirian High Council? What is your higher purpose?

We are a delegation of light beings of the Galactic Federation holding frequency at the sixth density, and ours is a group of 144 representatives which includes:

* Illuminated earth souls
* Ascended Sirians from Satais (of these, we are three primary
  Speakers working through our channel, Trydjya)
* Christed Extraterrestrials
* Ascended Dolphin Beings and the Great Whales
* Ascended Masters (The Overseers)
* Angelic beings (The Guardians)
* Masters of the Aghartan Leadership

Our purpose is to elevate consciousness of the multiverse in which
we take part, serving where we can and gleaning what we can
of what lies before us. Those who precede us, in turn, help lead us
into the bright light.

So is the eternal process of soul climbing higher in the journey of infinite return, a process without beginning and without
end.

*In these past few years there has been much opening to the Sirian
information. Why us, why now?*

Light beings of Sirius have long been working with the human
race: from your seeding, through the earliest generations of
Atlantis ... to present day.

Our communications are accentuated at various key evolutionary points of human development, leading up to this extraordinary time of your Solar Deity's ascension.

We have appeared in physical form on Earth as human
"starseed," for we do know how to retrograde into the lower den-

sities and rewire the intelligence codes—the DNA—so that we can hold frequency there, in the density, as needed.

Sentinels of the light realms, we have come into your reality in dark times, bringing the flame of experience to light the soul of human spirit. We have come in times of enormous quantum leaps, as in the birth of Egypt, where we were celebrated as gods and goddesses of ancient pantheons. We have appeared in the caves, the mountains, the valleys of the Earth Keepers, and always, at every point in your evolutionary journey, we have loved you unconditionally.

Our love is constant and unending.

However, we no longer have to slow our individual evolutionary journeys to serve humankind, by making ourselves present in form, as we have in other moments of human experience. It is no longer necessary, for your passing through the photon belt and the imminent passage of Earth through the astral cord of Ra have refined your vibrational fields so acutely that we are now beginning to reach you in the etheric, appearing to you at the sacred vortices of Earth's electromagnetic outer body and speaking to you through the selected channels.

Since the turning of the millennium at 2000 (by your Western calendar), we are accelerating our contact with the human race—and with the animals, for they, too, are in urgent need of assistance.

Did something specific occur at that time to facilitate this expanded contact with us?

Yes. At the turning of the millennium, marked by your calendar at midnight of 1999, a monumental event took place, causing a tidal wave of light to wash over human consciousness and establishing a new field of oscillating currents to pass between us.

Sirius passed directly over the Egyptian Giza meridian at that precise moment of Earth's time line, whereby your clocks struck the closing of the 24th hour—activating the Great Octahedron, which you know as the Great Pyramid at Giza.

This was written in the Akashic Record—it was determined many many millennia past that it would occur just this way. And it was so.

What effect did the passing of Sirius at that appointed hour have upon the Secret Government's plan to place a gold cap atop the Great Pyramid?

It raised the vibration of that vortex to such a peak that the project could not proceed and the energies inherent in the intention behind it were transmuted and defused. The electromagnetic energy flow lines of the activated Octahedron (the Great Pyramid in its entirety) protected it from any interference.

Indeed, the Great Octahedron of Giza was emitting such an unfathomable frequency at that point on the time-space continuum that it actually had the capacity to shatter gold. This was Divine Intervention.

This, the master switch of Gaia's energy body, is simply not accessible to the dark force, no matter how diligent their efforts to activate it. They cannot find the way, for it is through the heart of Gaia, from whom they have alienated themselves completely, utterly, and without remorse.

Why? What would have happened had it been allowed to proceed?

The probable outcome of that act, or shall we say the power elite's intention, was to decelerate Earth's resonant frequency, by altering the time lines of your planet. It was a necessary part of the Annunaki's ongoing and desperate plan to lower the planet's vibration into a dull harmonic with Nebiru, establishing the linkage needed to bring Nebiru through the ascension cords of your Sun.

They failed. Or rather, as we have intimated to you, they were not allowed to proceed.

The Great Octahedron, activated, is the ultimate time machine. Those of you who have entered there with us have experienced the shift of time and space and know of what we speak.

Your explanation of the Annunaki intention to lasso Earth in order to drag the remote planet of Nebiru into our solar system was mind-boggling and difficult to embrace as a possibility in the laws of physics that govern the Universe.

Please can you elaborate this essential point of the teachings.

The "laws of physics," or rather your perception of the workings of the material universe, are based upon your three-dimensional perception of reality—which, you are now learning, may very well be mistaken.

With the exception of those brilliant new philosophers and scientists who have defied the conventionalists and are thinking "out-of-the-box" of conformity, your teachers of universal para-digms and mechanics are still attempting to confine the abstrac-tion of the unknown to very tightly regulated concepts of how the physical universe works.

They are just barely capable of running the brush over the canvas of possibilities, where the incredibly complex design of the multiverse can become visible to the mind's eye.

We hear your endless debates about the beginnings of the Uni-verse and the source of life within it. There is no end to humankind's search for answers to the unknown: some believe in a Prime Creator, source of the intelligent design of life through-out the Universe. Others (the "Big Bang" theorists) adhere to the concept of arbitrary causality, for they have yet to reconcile their views of just what existed before the "great explosion" from which the physical universe emerges, expands, and eventually dies into their imaginings of a cold expanse of nothingness.

Yet others conceive of the human experience as some form of subjective repentance, believing that you are all wandering souls on a cluttered highway of sin and evil, driven to defy a judgmen-tal god who observes and evaluates your every sinful thought and illicit action—preparing to cast you into the dark caves of hell: the Big Brother theory deified!

Others still adhere to purely clinical ideas of the so-called "laws of physics" that have been defined by your great thinkers of gen-erations past and refined to be more far-reaching in scope, in line with the expanding technological advances of your twenty-first century.

Yet, despite the endless layers of interpretation, the technolog-ical advances, the debate and experimentation, your societies, on

the whole, have remained completely perplexed by (if not igno-
rant of) the nature of the conscious universe.

Only now, as you approach the greatest shift any planetary
body can experience, are you beginning to understand that reality is conscious thought; that thought travels in waves; that these
waves resonate at certain frequencies; and so on—that the multidimensional Universe is a sea of constantly vibrating strings of
consciousness with unlimited expressions and manifestations, in
countless dimensions and parallel worlds.

As for your question: can the Nebiruans actually lasso the
Earth to achieve their end? Let us say that such a possibility was
far more feasible before the millennium eve, when the capping
of the Great Octahedron of Giza was aborted.

We read that now, more than ever before, the vibratory signature of the planet Nebiru simply cannot reach resonance with
Earth, which, despite appearances and the maneuvers of the dark
forces at work on your planet, is rising.

*When I read your material regarding how the Annunaki exist and
how they have created military installations inside the Martian terrain, one very troubling thought occurred to me. Will Mars be ascending and, if so, will we be faced with them in the next dimension?
After what we have been through, I can't bear the thought that the
struggle continues in the next dimension.*

The Annunaki exist on Earth—and Earth is ascending. Why
should it worry you any more to know that they are burrowed
into the subsurface layers of Mars, also ascending?

We ask you to remember that no matter what expression of

disharmony confronts you, you are capable of rising above it and then, as a true lightworker, you serve to help heal it.

You can face them at home, on Mars, on the physical, on the etheric: as long as you do not allow fear to cast its dark shadow on your soul. When you are in your heart center, you serve as a lighthouse for the lost and in ways you still may not totally understand your light reaches them. It helps to diffuse their intention and assist them, at the soul level, to seek higher ground.

To answer your question more specifically:

The planet Mars is home not only to the Annunaki, although we acknowledge they do have military installations there. In the Martian underground there are found other native civilizations, the contemporary generations whose ancestors built the cities and sacred sites that have been observed in your now famous images of the Cydonia landscape and—although you may yet find it difficult to believe—there are also installations of human beings living in highly cultivated, incredibly developed underground cities.

The Mars reality is so very much a projection of Earth as it would appear in the physical reality in a future existence, were it destined to remain in the third dimension of physical density.

Observing what little you are shown of Martian topography, it must have occurred to you that this planet (which you are now discovering for its true history) is the quintessential model of an intelligent species' abuse of planetary energies.

Surely you recognize (or, at the very least, contemplate) that it is a place where the prevailing intelligent life forms consumed the planet's resources, just as humankind now devastates your own. They destroyed their atmosphere, as you are destroying the atmosphere of your own planet, and finally went underground to survive.

The destruction of the biosphere is the way of unenlightened civilizations on countless planets—it is Nebiru, it is Mars, and yes, it is Earth in progress. It is the reflection of the duality of the third dimension, where technological "advancement" of civilizations inevitably leads to isolation and separateness from nature and which, conversely, marks its decline.

Know that what little you are being shown of the Mars explorations and the events unfolding on that planet is a mirage. The reality of what goes on there—both on the surface and within—is far more complex.

Never forget that much of what filters down to the human population is crafted and designed information intended to hold you in ignorance, until those who currently (appear to) hold the power decide or are forced to reveal the truth to you.

We do understand that all the planets of your solar system have been linked and prepared for passage, including Mars: your futuristic reflection.

The truth of extraterrestrial life, particularly within your own solar system, is soon to be revealed and all of you will know the splendor of contact. We assure you there is nothing to fear from your distant cousins and that countless wonders await you all at the reunion.

The Annunaki of Mars, whom you so dread, will be more or less the same as those known to you on Earth. Nothing more. Nothing less.

You do know how they operate and you are learning to identify them.

They, too, are driven by survival instinct; they, too, search for the solution of their planet's plight as earth scientists now begin contemplating colonization of space as the solution to humankind's exploitation and destruction of Earth's habitats. That is the clear reason, you understand, that your governments are sneaking about on the Martian surface.

Can you tell us what other planets in our solar system host intelligent life?

After what we have just said, you should not be surprised to hear that all of the planets of Ra bear life, as do most of the moons that rotate those planets. As intelligence exists in the consciousness of all life, we do declare to you that intelligent life fills the immediate environment—your solar family—as it does the entire Universe.

Always remember that the planets, themselves, are living, conscious beings.

Your own moon, Luna, is buzzing with various life forms, including human beings, who frequent the bases there on the dark side—where they are out of reach of all Earth-based surveillance technologies.

Why have there been no communications between the planets in our solar system? Surely, at this point in the evolution of our Sun, there should have been at least radio signals or some form of communication—no?

There are indeed communications! You are simply not privy to that information for, as we have told you before, the Power does not think you are ready to receive the reality of extraterrestrial life and so you are not allowed access to their secret files.

You have not been "allowed" until now, that is. However, soon—very soon now—the undeniable proof will be laid before you and nothing will be able to stop you, the human race, from knowing.

Not even the most skeptical of nonbelievers will be able to deny the reality of intelligent life from beyond your tiny planet.

Radio signals do indeed abound in your solar system. Bear in mind that Earth is an extremely noisy planet and getting louder every moment you hold your place in the universe of matter!

Although it is difficult for the scientific teams to define and isolate extraterrestrial signals from the infinity of frequencies that fill your own orbit, interfering with their equipment and hence limiting their ability to interpret what is being beamed out from other celestial beings ... they do exist!

They have been identified.

The SETI and META astronomy projects under way in your scientific communities have captured what they have deemed potential "artificial" radio signals from just outside of the planet Saturn; from Jupiter they have identified three bands of radio transmissions from the planet that are identified as coming from the surface, from the plasma body that links Jupiter with its moon, Io, and from the magnetic field that encircles Io. There are also signals from Neptune now being studied that indicate the same.

What we are telling you is that there are constant candidate signals being detected through your SETI program that more than meet the requirements for transmissions of alien intelligence and, moreover, we are quite confident that someone there on Planet Earth is, indeed, responding. ...

Remember, too, that the planetary bodies of your star system speak to each other, share energy fields, and exchange the love that permeates the Cosmos.

Are you also in communication with the intelligent life on these planets?

Yes, but, as we have stated before, we of the Council are currently primarily concerned with the human race that populates Gaia. There is, however, great interest in the higher spheres regarding the ascension of your Sun and assistance is being directed to all the living of your realm.

Soon (in your lifetimes) you will enjoy interplanetary contact. This we have repeatedly affirmed to you.

So much is about to unfold upon which you can only speculate (in your fantasies of a future that seems impossible to you now) and yet it is the "right now" of your experience.

Other ascended extraterrestrials—such as the Pleiadians and the Arcturians—are more actively involved with your sister deities and the preparation of the intelligent beings on those planetary bodies, although they do speak to humankind. It is always a matter of attunement—of resonance—and there is no limitation to where the harmonies in the great symphony of life will be found in the Music of the Spheres.

Can you explain to us more precisely what you mean by the Music of the Spheres? I first came across this term in your teachings and have since seen reference to it in the Pythagorean teachings ... but I still do not completely understand.

The universe of matter and its holographic parallel universes are all interconnected in complex, exquisite cosmometric forms that are the sacred works of Creation. These form a magnificently articulated lattice of mathematical proportions and spatial relationships and ratios that comprise the fiber of many levels of reality and hence it is still quite an abstraction for you to imagine. Nothing is disproportionate or haphazard in the Universe; all is in perfect harmony—all is interdependent, unified, **One**.

Around every celestial body there is a unique and breathtakingly beautiful sacred design of a crystalline formation—a cosmometric blueprint—where all is in constant evolution upward, in a linear sense, in the light of soul seeking perfection.

This divine holographic framework is in perpetual motion, endlessly spinning to the master rhythm of all Creation.

The spinning of these crystalline structures creates a master note for each celestial body. We refer to this as the "wam" frequency. It propels the very spin of the planets, moons, and yes, even stars.

It is the same within each of you. The spin of the energy wheels of your own energy networks and your merkabic fields set the music of your soul—your unique sound coding.

Each soul essence in the Cosmos is surrounded by its own complex crystalline grid. Every soul has its major key, its special note ... that which we have described to you as the "wam" vibration.

The ability to perceive the Music of the Spheres is a gift acquired by the Masters amongst you who have traveled far along the path to spiritual enlightenment.

I have read that Sirian mother ships are currently surrounding the Earth, preparing to evacuate large numbers of human beings to safety. Can you confirm this?

Dear one, we ask you to take a deep breath and then ask yourself this: what is it you are to be saved from? If you are referring to the Earth Changes now in full evolution on your planet, we remind you that this alteration of the climate—the seas and the land formations—is every bit a part of Gaian evolution (reflection of your Sun's acceleration) as it is your individual and collective karmic manifestation.

If, indeed, you have progressed to the point that you understand how your individual thoughts, acts, and emotions contribute to the collective consciousness and how the collective creates the holographic universe, you will be far closer to perceiving and comprehending how that which is unfolding before you is yours and remains with you ... until you alter the vibration.

Your individual attention to healing your immediate environment and contributing what you can to raising global consciousness has everything to do with your future relationship with Earth on the fourth dimension.

Remember: You cannot escape karma.

You can release it, yes.

You can heal it, alter it, accelerate or delay it ... but there is no escaping it.

We ask, too, that you consider how any alien force could possibly remove enough of you from the planet to save you. How, do you believe, would the selection process be made? Would the "good" people be taken away in ships, while the "bad" be left to perish?

Would you truly go, blindly, with the so-called saviors—never looking back at a world you helped to destroy?

Perhaps this is a fantasy of the ruling elite of your planet, but we assure you it is not the reality.

Surely you recognize old patterns and thought programs in such "judgment day" scenarios. We ask you not to create new religions around the future of extraterrestrial contact, at a time when you are about to release yourselves from the imposed dogma of value systems in which you are forever attempting to escape your guilt and be absolved of your sin—in order to "make the grade."

In the density of the physical universe or as collective consciousness on higher states of existence, any and all evolved alien civilizations understand that your planet is about to experience a most magnificent journey and that, despite appearances, you are blessed to be there on Earth, right now—in the thick of it.

You, ancient soul, have chosen to be there. No evolved alien civilization would attempt to intervene or interrupt the process of your passage and will only be intent upon assisting you—at the soul level. You have incarnated now in order to take part in this monumental celestial transition and you are right on track, in the home stretch.

Trust in the wisdom of the higher self.

Were an extraterrestrial force to pluck you out of the reality into which you intentionally chose to materialize, it would be a true deterrent to your soul intent, would it not?

What remains to be considered is whether or not you will raise your vibration to the point that you do indeed experience ascension in full conscious awareness—or rather, as will be the case of those entrained to the lower frequencies, you will choose to remain bound to the wheel of karmic return.

That is your choice to make.

It always has been.

And forever will it be.

An entity by the name of Yahweh, an ancient being who is aligned with the Zeta Reticulans and an advanced race known as the Traders, has stated that the Sirians have been punished in the past for adversely affecting human evolution. Is this true?

We do not know of this race "Traders" nor do we acknowledge the Zeta Reticulans to be a spiritually "advanced" civilization and let us suggest that you question the source of your entity.

Many are the wandering astral beings seeking audience with the vulnerable and the ego-centered of lower dimensions. We ask you, once again, to listen to any and all information that comes to you through your heart and to use discernment about the sources of that information.

As to the question posed here: if there is to be punishment for any act taken with the intention of serving the highest good of the other, then it can only be defined as "creating karmic chains" that slow the progress of both.

We have recognized the karma created by our intervention and are working through it by serving **without intervening** and assisting the human race.

As for the question of punishment: know that no outside force can impose upon the karmic process of one or the many. Karma is simply the result of an action, individual or collective, as taught to you most succinctly in the Buddhist tradition.

2

Into the Fourth Dimension

We hear your question ringing out to us: "What will it be like to leave the Earth and ascend to the fourth dimension?" To begin with, we hope we have made clear to you the fact that Earth moves through as an ascending celestial body, so that you are still earth-centered in the higher dimension. In essence, you won't leave Gaia ... you will mutate with her.

You worry about form; we can tell you that much of your perception will be so subtly altered that you will barely recognize that you are no longer in the physical.

Those of you who choose to ascend the spiral as earth residents will still be confronted with Gaia, as she recovers from the extremes of human abuse and disharmony, and you will be dedicating much of your thoughts and energies to healing her. You will still love, emote, and experience life in many ways as you do at this point of your development, but there will be many shades of change in your awareness ... many, many changes, indeed.

You are working towards becoming masters of your realities, extracting yourselves from the exoteric structures that dominate and manipulate you. Now, more than ever, you need to rely upon your own perceptions and accumulated experience to move through your new realities. The Eve (your intuitional awareness) will take center stage and most of your impressions will come through that aspect. The Adam (your logical mind) will relax, yielding once again to Eve ... letting the intuition override the logic. Earth will evolve as well, as the disharmony that she brings through the black hole will begin (by definition) to heal, for without your egos, separation, and extreme emotions, you will come quite rapidly to harmony with Gaia.

The exoteric rulers, those who have directed you into obedience and fear, will most likely remain entrapped in the third dimension, experiencing the death process which will occur over large portions of your planet and incarnating on other celestial bodies of the physical universe at other times. Of these, some will join the power elite, those direct descendants of the Annunaki, as they move into the void of the grey zone. And you, the awakening, will transmute from the physical realm into your new experience of life as the interpenetrating of mind and events, where you will blend into the vibration of all the elements of consciousness in simultaneous existence.

Will you have physical bodies? Fear not, you will not lose your identities in the next phase! Do you understand what we intend by "light bodies"? Your temples, the bodies that house your soul essence, will have been raised to higher frequencies, and that will bring new points of reference to your self-awareness, your perception of others, and your ability to recognize the cosmic waves that are passing through you. You will perceive each other's energies as vibrational fields, knowing in an instant the emotional and mental states of the other. You will be telepathic, free to communicate without words, which are, in fact, limitations in your current experience.

We believe that, by now, you have accepted that our instrument brings a council of extra-planetary beings through to you on these pages. If not, you would already have put away this book. But is it the printed word or our vibrational codes that you are actually reading? Trydjya, a conscious energy being, does not simply perform as a robot, bringing our rhetoric through her fingertips and into her computer. A consciousness unit, she experiences our thoughts in a form of telepathic synergy; she sees images as we transmit those waves across the screen of her third-eye vision, and then, as a physical being of your realm, condenses into words that which is our intended meaning.

She is gifted ... so are you, for within all conscious beings lies the potential of expansion and higher awareness. It is simply a matter of developing your skills and trusting the voice of your higher selves—your guidance—that determines how soon you, too, will open to receive the frequencies, and that is part and process of your development.

In the fourth dimension, these skills become your common tools and you will all be opening, like fields of wildflowers feverishly bursting in the bloom of Spring. There will still exist degrees of awareness, for your individual abilities are only as developed as your soul is evolved. Your gifts are the rewards that you have earned through your spiritual accomplishments and the resolution of karmic debt. This is true of all dimensions and realities in the Cosmos, as we understand them. Just as you must face and overcome adversity in your process, so must you know the gratification of achievement, for these are the guidelines that show you the pathway home.

We know that you are looking for a practical, detailed picture of your future experience in the higher dimensions, and that, despite the wealth of knowledge being made available to you now, there is still much allusion and little factual information regarding just what you are moving towards. Be patient. Remember that if you were to know all things before experiencing them, there would be no purpose to their acquisition. If you were to know the destination in its entirety, would you be so anxious to embark upon the journey? Anticipation of discovery is your greatest motivation, for, once you break away from divinity, you begin the education process and you never stop learning—not even upon your return to The All That Is, That Ever Was, and That Always Will Be. Understand that, in returning, you bring your acquired knowledge back into the All, and that was your intention from the very beginning.

Those of you who are about to enter the four-dimensional states of consciousness have been accepted into the Institute of Higher Learning ... Initiates in the experiential school of awareness. Having made the grade, you have earned many rewards, and we can tell you that if you have not already begun to see, you will soon experience clairvoyant vision, for you will be seeing with the psychic eye, just as you will be hearing without physical ears and feeling without touch.

If you are already blessed with these gifts, you will soon notice your abilities have intensified, for that is simply the natural process, where all moves up. Your heightened senses become that much more acute as you proceed, for as you have been operating for some time on higher levels, you simply go higher. You have much to look forward to, for you already know a lot about vibrational fields, thought emanations, and etheric energies. You will be passing in and out of the fourth dimension with ease, reconnecting with your teachers and guides on even higher planes.

The Cosmos of Soul

You have explained to us that the fourth dimension is where time is no longer the illusion it is in the third dimension and I am having great difficulty perceiving this reality.

Can you help me get a handle on this, so that it is not so mental— but rather, can you help create a visual sense of how we will exist without time?

Consider that in your intellectual understanding of time, you are totally trapped in linear concepts—for that is how you operate with logical mind.

When you daydream, or dream, or meditate, or astral journey, you are slipping right out of the dimension and moving around on other planes, not recognizing that you exist simultaneously in both the third, where you are momentarily anchored in biological form, and the others, wherever you find resonance.

Imagine this:

It is a brilliant, sun-blessed day and you have decided to go running in the field. Returning, you twist your ankle and fall to the ground, the pain surging through your body.

A nearby neighbor witnesses the accident. She runs to the house and returns to you with a pack of frozen water, which she understands is the best treatment for the swelling and, as you lie there with the ice positioned over the joint, you feel significant relief—while your physical body alters its form in reaction to the traumatic event.

How this occurs, again, is an example of the "resonance principle" that underlines our teachings. Quite simply, the slow-moving water molecules in their frozen state communicate the cosmometric designs of their slowed frequency and the love of the one nurturing you to the frenetic molecules in the heated waters of the traumatized joint, slowing the vibration and so reducing the swelling.

The ice is also interacting with your own highly focused intent to ease the pain and reduce the swelling, for as you well know— water is conscious and it reacts to your thought projections instantaneously.

Soon (with "time"), the ice melts in the warmth of the sun and returns to its pre-frozen form of liquid water. It becomes absorbed first by the towel in which it is held, then runs down your ankle and onto the grass: some being absorbed in the earth; some evaporating upon your skin in the warmth of the sun.

As you check inside the towel you see that the ice has turned to water; as you observe your ankle and foot you see the water has turned to vapor and then it is gone.

But is it?

Hasn't that, too, involved transformation of matter, as the liquid form of the H_2O has now been released into the atmosphere—"evaporated," as you term it—to become part of the atmospheric content, adding (in an admittedly limited way) moisture to the air?

We ask you to contemplate the significance of this transformational process and make the comparison to your own existence in simultaneous time, where you understand that you **are** the water, the ice, and the vapor ... you are the moisture in the air.

This is a simplistic example of simultaneous time, somewhat removed, conceptually, from the linear constraints of your present understanding.

Can you speak to us more precisely about the warping of time as we approach the point of ascension? How is time being altered?

As you move more rapidly towards solar center, where you pass through the cord and into the next dimension, more of you are becoming acutely aware of how time is mutating. You experience time "flying," missing time, and a sense of its distortion as the hours, months, and years race past you ... as it seems they have never passed before.

This is not merely a "sensation," as you are led to believe, caused by the frenetic lifestyles of your contemporary societies. All is spinning faster as your Sun prepares for ascension, and this increased vibration is changing the galactic tones of your space in the physical universe.

With the new harmonics of your solar family accelerating, artificial time no longer holds the same values. You must consider how your concept of time and your measures of it are based on archaic perceptions of the interacting dynamics of the Earth, Moon, and Sun and how, if these celestial bodies are indeed altering their vibrational frequencies, then so is time, as you understand it, mutating as well.

We ask you to consider, as a second thought, how your individual biological clocks are accelerating as well and how all of this mutation is a sublime reflection of divinity at work.

If all are to ascend, won't we be taking all the current problems of Earth through to the fourth dimension to be solved there?

At no time have we declared to you that all will ascend. That is an incorrect conclusion. In the process of Earth Changes, the extremes that are occurring will vastly alter the population, as you begin to spin ever faster into the epicenter of the vortex.

Earth's shifting geophysical body has already begun to wreak havoc on your populations.

Some of the changes are a natural progression; some are deliberate, man-made violations of Gaian energy zones. Others are the manifestation of your species' utter disregard for the Earth; yet others have been the result of the unbridled technological exploitation of alien nations and their intervention in your planetary affairs.

Others still are the result of runaway technology that you have brought back from the "future," where you have simultaneous levels of consciousness and from where you retrieve the kinds of information that earth society is not yet evolved enough to use ethically, harmoniously, and with a sense of true proportion.

What we invite you to contemplate is how the lower vibrations of disharmony on your planet and the energies of those who are responsible for their emanations will surely not be able to hold frequency in the next dimension.

It can be best described by imagining a television station fading in and out of the screen, as one attempts to find the right coordinates with the antennae that will bring it in clearly.

Much (but not all) of that which is creating disturbance in your world at this time will simply not appear in the next realm. It will disintegrate in the wake of those higher frequencies and become mere dust, clinging to an imaginary lens on the no-time.

Other aspects of earth consciousness, where you are shown how your collective intent alters matter, will be a central aspect of your existence in that realm.

Then you are saying that those who have not refined their energies will not ascend. What will happen to them?

Those who prefer to attune to the lower vibrations and those with unresolved karma will most likely pass from the lifetime into another physical lifetime at some other place in the three-dimensional universe—as Earth will no longer exist on that plane. They will continue to experience the wheel of reincarnation, until they no longer need to work through the accumulated karma that binds them to the limitations of the holographic three-dimensional framework—the matrix.

There is a significant body of beings in your world that feeds of beastly incarnate pleasures, like ravenous wolves upon fresh-kill. These individuals are not at all interested in higher aware-ness; rather, they are committed to the various levels of sensate experience and gratification.

These strata of your societies will not come through and glad they are to move to other material realms, traveling the wheel of karmic return to a new destination, where tempting new carnal desires can be satiated.

So is their intention; so will they create it.

This, all of this, you will soon understand is a reflection of our process—we separate from Source, leap into the abyss, and then, having drunk to the very last hypnotic drop of the elixir of suffering and isolation—we take to the road of return, climbing out of the darkness and back into the light.

To each of us is known a time and a season from which we break through the chrysalis and spread our wings, gliding upon the softness of the heart breeze ... glistening in the light of Creation.

To ascend in the light body ... does this mean burning off the physical body as in "cleansing by fire" as prophesied for Earth: an extremely painful physical death?

The process of passing through Ra's ascension tube—the astral cord—will be so incredibly fast (faster than the speed of light itself) that it is understandably inconceivable to you now, intellectually, as it will be then, in the first stages of your passing.

It is not a death process.

It is not a painful one.

It is a most remarkable brilliance and then ... the awakening: illumination.

Hold a flashlight in your hand, pointing it directly at the wall. Click the switch. Faster than the speed of that light hitting and then illuminating that wall ... almost as fast as the thought of turning that switch: that will be the speed of your passage.

Before that ray of light can reach the wall, your entire solar system will have passed through the astral cords of Ra and entered the fourth dimension.

It will be that immediate!

We ask you to consider how one could experience pain in such an infinitesimal time frame and invite you to consider how that paradigm has been presented in prophecy to hold you, bent in obedience and glued to your terror.

Perhaps it is the seer's own fear and ignorance that constructs the witches' pyre as a paradigm for the so-named "cleansing" of form.

Some spiritual writings say that major religions will continue to exist for long periods of our time. Do you believe these religions will transcend to the fourth dimension?

Institutionalized religion, as it currently exists in your framework, will lose all of its contemporary value and meaning, once you lift the veils and recognize that the primary reason structured religions exist on your planet is to control you (on various levels), by dictating human behavior and thought.

Once you stand in the golden white light of Creation and know, without question, the immensity of such unconditional love, no interpretation or belief system will ever serve you again.

At this time of the renewed crusades on Earth, you are seeing how religion has been made to serve the political machinery that drives the disharmony of peoples and nations. It is being stripped of its higher intention and cast into the lowest form of mind control. It is now used as a justification to commit violent acts against the other, while corralling people into vast holding zones of obedience, manipulated hypocrisy, and righteousness.

Religions that organize you into prayer on one day and then convince you to kill the "enemy" on another have nothing to do with your connection to "God" (however perceived) and everything to do with mass persuasion and control.

True religion, which we prefer to define as "spiritual progression," is determined by your personal and group soul consciousness and the intention of each and the All—of Unity—to raise the flame of awareness, celebrating life and the beauty of all existence and serving the highest purpose of the entirety.

Neither bound to the mercilessness of a God who would punish you and ban you from ever entering the "gates of heaven," nor bent in terror of the all-illusive devil, who waits to clutch you from your sleep and rip your souls from your chests, you will see clearly how your thoughts create reality and how **being** light brings you **into** the Light.

Should we die before the major shift in 2012, would we be at our appointed destination already? I would not like to miss this magnificent event and all the preparation along with it.

Sweet soul, we repeat to you what we have said before: as a stream of consciousness you are learning that you are always where you are meant to be when you follow the flow and the current.

The soul shines the reflections of the light that ripples through the cosmic waves into your heart and you know, despite your fear, that the time of leaving a given lifetime is determined well before entering. There is nothing arbitrary nor is anything left to chance about the time of your departure—just as there is nothing random about your entry.

You know it and have made peace with it at the soul level. Remember that the soul purpose was clearly defined before you crystallized into matter, entering the physical realm, and that most of those of you who are even aware of the shift are those who most likely have chosen to participate, to assist Gaia, and to serve in that process.

Although it often appears as random, unexpected, cruel, and unselective, death is preordained by the soul. Your entering the physical realm (that which you may term "incarnating") and your exiting are determined at the time the soul leaves the Halls of Learning and prepares for the new life.

Despite appearances, nothing is "accidental" in the theater of life, however convincing is the illusion that life happens "to you."

We can tell you that many will pass before the process begins, for countless souls walking the earth at this time are not prepared for ascension, nor do they believe in such evolutionary milestones.

Of these, there are some who will slip into the grey zone; others who will choose to reincarnate at other locations in the material universe; others still who will travel the spiral at a snail's pace—as is appropriate to their soul process.

Be fearless, trusting that the higher self knows exactly where it need be and that the soul is clear for take-off, majestically awaiting its turn on the runway to the stars.

About the grey zone: When, why, and for how long do spirits experience it?

In the simplest terms available to us, we describe the grey zone as the closest thing to nonexistence that exists in the Universe. It is the in-between, where those souls that are simply unwilling to progress (either by returning back into the density of matter to learn those lessons that need mastering or by progressing upward along the spiral of light) and those who take their own lives remain in a sort of timeless glue, where almost all vibration ceases to penetrate and where the light barely filters through the density ...

Through the mist there is a hint of light, of sound, of vibration—but it appears to be so far away as to be unreachable to those wandering about, perennially lost in the vaporous void.

It has been identified in many of your religious texts, however elusive in their depiction of the grey zone: the Duat, Purgatory ... all, in some aspects, attempt to describe the zone, which crosses the path of the soul, as it progresses in and out of physical reality.

There, too, are lost souls (shall we say "entrapped" ones), who seek to release themselves by attaching to those who are passing over. Therein lies the danger described in your mystical teachings.

Many are those who come into physical reality weighted by souls who have "hitched" a ride in order to be pulled from the greyness. Not until they are able to release the attachment are these carriers freed of the burden of the soul who has ridden in and until that moment the vibrations of the "hitchhiker" can dramatically alter those of the carrier.

All too often (as is the case with those diagnosed as suffering from multiple personality disorder), it is more than one!

This is far more common than you would imagine and so detrimental to the individual's journey. It is not that, in this process, the soul carrying the cling-on serves to assist that one. Rather, the unresolved soul/spirit that has attached itself imposes its frequency upon the other, entraining the carrier to its own vibratory fields, and both are pulled down, into the ambiguity of unresolved karma and lower consciousness.

With what you know of karma, you can imagine how this connection can link the two (or more) and how detrimental it can be for all involved.

Far too many souls, lost in the grey zone, seem to never find their way out, to release from the infinite search for the light—however, this is not the case. We remind you that all consciousness eventually moves towards the light. The lost, the shadow, the darkness—all eventually moves into the light. That is the nature of existence ... the one absolute Truth that we feel we can speak without hesitation. All is in perennial movement upwards on the spiral of light.

Other frequenters of the grey zone, such as the grey technicians, are assisted by the forces of darkness, who occasionally manage to open a portal there in the misty vacuum. However, this is quite the exception.

Unfortunately, they are pulled back into the darkness, retrograding back onto the downward spiral ... until they have resolved the karma that has linked them to those vibrations and finally—eventually—find their way back to the spiral of light: the way home.

Remember that Prime Creator exists everywhere, in all things—even the grey zone reflects the design of Prime Creator for all conscious evolution.

The grey zone—a parallel reality—can envelop planets, entire solar systems, even galaxies: wherever the vibratory patterns are such that the deity itself chooses not to progress. This can be described as a result of the overall consciousness of the deity's inhabitants and life forms.

Is this grey zone the same space where souls exiting Earth are found—those who remain attached to a place or person here?

This is a "grey" area! Know that, as the soul passes from the physical and pierces the veil, it is capable of viewing and interacting with the environment that it has left for a number of reasons.

These have to do with unfinished details and unresolved injustices—or simply the outpouring of love for the suffering and the grieving of those who have been left behind.

Trapped souls, instead, are bound to the illusion of their physical lives with such intensity that they do not make the passage and hence remain in the hinterlands we have described.

These are the ghostly spirits that walk the halls of ancient days, searching for (but never finding) a way out of their haze and they are entrapped in the torturous memories that bind them, like glue, to the nowhere of the grey zone.

How can they be freed, if ever, from their torment?

Skilled clairvoyants and sensitives, capable of perceiving these spirits, can often create and sustain a high enough vibrational field that, for a moment, enough light enters to create an escape tunnel for these light-deprived souls to follow.

This can be a dangerous experiment in the hands of the inexperienced, particularly those who still have not resolved the illusions and fantasies of ego consciousness, who then find they have created a karmic bond with the spirit. Some become carriers for these spirits and are then subject to various forms of invasive energies known as "attachments" and these are often extremely difficult to release from, once they have found their vehicle— their host.

Please do not misinterpret our message: we are not recommending this level of astral work to those who have not been called to serve in this capacity, nor to those who have not had substantial training in working with astral entities.

To those of you who have been called, we remind you to detach yourselves completely in service to the highest good of the All and to prepare the space with light shields, grounding techniques, and higher astral assistance before embarking on such journeys into the shadow lands.

Does the grey zone ascend, along with our star, into a lighter state of existence with our passage into the fourth dimension?

The grey zone is not an aspect of your Solar Deity—it is a parallel reality, somehow between the dimensions. It is not affected by the ascension of a star system.

Therefore, once the Earth (a three-dimensional planetary body) has passed through the vortex, only its imprint will remain in the ethers—but those entrapped spirits will remain bound to those earthly conditions that they created while in the physical lifetime, unless they receive assistance from conscious beings intent upon releasing them.

All remains in the ethers.

According to our master physicist, Einstein, nothing travels faster than the speed of light. How are we to account for your theory that, during our passage through the ascension cords, we will actually sur-pass the speed of light, defying physics?

As brilliant as the adept Einstein was during his time in body, we understand that many of his theories, however respected, were unproven. Therefore, they were not, in fact, resolved in the strictest interpretation of scientific "validation"—were they?

The scientific philosophers who have now begun to explore the possibility of strings of interwoven universes are moving beyond the Einstein vision, presenting the academic community with new and very exciting paradigms that are catching up with the spiritual understanding of cosmic order and the nature of reality.

It is known to the scientific world that subatomic particles can bi-locate to exist, simultaneously, at different points in the space-time continuum and that they can communicate instantaneously, defying the speed of light.

For example, we do observe experiments now being performed in your scientific communities whereby a sample of one's body fluids (the saliva) is observed under the microscope, while the donor has since left and traveled some distance from the laboratory. Amazed researchers are finding that the sample reacts to events provoking emotional responses within the donor miles away—and that these occur and are sustained for significant lengths of time.

The cells observed react simultaneously, as the events play out in mental and emotional fields of the physically distant donor.

As new understandings of the nature of reality emerge, you are learning how to prove and record how consciousness travels faster than light.

Thought is not limited to the third dimension—it is beyond time. It is instantaneous, simultaneous, all-pervading.

Thought and the focused, conscious intent travel through the cord to the other side of your co-existing higher vibratory, multidimensional self.

As you master the power of focused consciousness, you will recognize how you can reconstruct matter, where you intend—simply by directing your thought to that framework and then reassembling the resonant subatomic particles at that frequency to your specific coordinates.

Voilà! You manifest your conscious design in this way.

You do have the ability to accomplish this exercise and you do indeed bi-locate energetically quite regularly, but most of you are still too blinded by the illusions of three-dimensional reality to understand how that occurs at the unconscious (or shall we say unfocused) level.

Therefore, it is a far greater challenge for you to understand how you can create it at the conscious or focused level.

While you go about, distracted by your daily business in the maze of illusion—your soul perpetually creates the perfection and the template for your biological being to manifest in the density of the dimension in which you currently reside.

You move about on many levels, bringing every kind of experience into your mental and emotional bodies, and are usually relatively unaware of just what you are creating!!

In the fourth dimension, you will be fully conscious of your manifestations and hence, fully aware of what you create on every level.

Will there be a parallel three-dimensional world where problems not resolved before ascension will continue to be worked on?

There exist infinite parallel worlds. Imagine your image as it appears in a mirror—the illusion of what you look like as a physical being. If the mirror falls and breaks into many smaller pieces and you look again, your image appears in every shard. Each is a hologram of the big picture.

In an overly simplified manner, this is emblematic of the multidimensional Universe. Reflections of your world exist, like countless bits of fractured mirror, across the cosmic infinity: the vast physical universe and all the Great Beyond.

Will all of our sister planets and moons ascend with us?

That is something we cannot know with certainty, as there are many probable realities that co-exist in every moment of experience. However, we can tell you that it appears that the alignments have been set so that all proceed through as one, at a time when the events in your realm sound out in the Music of the Spheres like a Great Overture.

Know that the spacing of relative distances between the planets follows natural diatonic scale musical proportions ... and that there are similar harmonies, at every level, throughout the galaxy.

Such cosmometric proportions are the fabric of the Universe— they are the sheet music, if you will, of the symphony of Creation.

All the celestial beings in all dimensions, including Sirius, are the manifestations of music, frozen, in a very liberal sense, in space.

What will happen to the Annunaki puppets and the puppeteers who currently control Gaia?

From what we understand of the earth-based Annunaki, they do truly believe that they can successfully entrain Earth to the Nebiruan vibration and bring that planet into the fourth dimension with you—where they no doubt imagine themselves triumphant rulers of a world delivered unto a new paradigm.

Incapable of truly imagining the vibratory essence of the next density, where such dark maneuverings as theirs cannot cling, they remain unwavering in their robotic conviction that they must save the ancient world of Nebiru by anchoring that planet to Earth. They see this as the last hope for their dying home planet.

Upon your planet they hold tenuous rule—but rule they do . . . for the moment. They have resources. They have mastership of technology and cunning design.

They believe in the illusions of heroism, new worlds to conquer, and the type of fantasy that you have heard played so often as the "winner takes all" design behind their violence wars and global tyranny.

What we anticipate happening to the dark warriors is that they will crawl back into their underground cities and bunkers when you are nearing passage, the dream of Nebiru defeated, but still hoping to save themselves (at the very least) by hiding away in the underground of the planet, as it passes through the golden cord of Ra in ascension.

Although they have no true idea of the process of ascension and the subsequent mutation of matter, they do ardently cling to their conviction that they can "survive" and make it to the fourth dimension, riches in hand, to start anew.

In some ways they are very Egyptian in their perception of "taking it with them."

They will not.

Unfortunately, they have bound themselves to an inestimable journey upon the wheel of reincarnation, in the extreme density of the darkest physical space, and, very possibly, they will have to work through that karma for many lifetimes to come.

What exactly was happening with Anu and her inhabitants before, during, and after the collapse of Satais? Is or was the star system of Anu inhabited by the same kind of races, of the same origins, as the ones then living on Sothis and Satais?

Anu, the stellar deity, was nurturer to five celestial beings bearing intelligent life. Of these there was a wealth of bio-diversity ranging from the most complex aquatic creatures, the galactic ancestors of the Dolphin Beings, with the capacities of highly evolved and technologically superior societies.

Nebiru, on the other hand, spawned life forms that were more reptilian in nature; however, there, too, were and still are found highly sophisticated technological environments.

There was great intercultural exchange amongst many of the planetary bodies that shared the trilogy of light that was the Sisterhood of Sirius in the third dimension and we remind you that it still remains in a multidimensional context: Sirius A (Sothis) currently holding physical space in the third dimension; Sirius B

(Satais) resonating at sixth-dimensional frequencies; and Sirius C (Anu) at the fourth density.

If that is true, then, aren't we going to be resonating with Nebiru in the next dimension? What does all of this mean for us and our ongoing struggle with the Annunaki?

Nebiru, you recall, did not ascend with the star. It remains in the third dimension, currently passing through the darkness of space from Sirius A on its trajectory back to your solar system.

As for the Annunaki, you will soon realize that, as you proceed ahead into lighter densities, you will be called upon to reach out a hand and help them, even them, to climb the spiral stairway. All will progress. All will eventually move into the light. You will see so clearly how your helping those lost in the dark tunnels accelerates your own journey.

Will you continue to fear them, then, or will you forgive them, sending the love you hold for the light into the darkness?

It is up to you to transmute the energy and this is every bit a part of your Initiation as it is your mastery of the New Frontier.

As I have a young daughter, I fear for the children. What is to become of them?

Blessed are you for being a caretaker of a child. You have been given one of the greatest joys of life, but your fear will diminish that joy and therefore you will be greatly benefited, as will she, when you let it go.

Many of those coming in now are ancient souls who have come to take an active part in the magnificence unfolding. They come from many parallel universes and yes, even other dimensions, to serve and to assist the life forms of your beautiful planet ... and they know exactly what to do.

They are fearless until they learn fear. It pours through your milk, your essence, your entire being.

That which you fear the most, ironically, you create for your child: the suffering that emanates from you, the nurturing mother, and imprints itself upon her consciousness. It is a weighty burden—your own fear of the unknown—that she may possibly have to carry forward for you ... forever.

If anything, this sweet soul may very well have come in to extend a hand to you when you feel you have lost the way, for she is very likely to have prepared to serve on levels you may not yet understand.

Many old souls have earned the right (of their own karmic clearing) to come in at the moment of transition: they come along for the ride, in a sense. They come in with their eyes open, pulsating with the exhilaration of what lies just ahead of them, so near to the vortex point that they can go through it with the innocence of their young life experience (however brief in your earthly sense), rather than with the fear that is acquired in your long adult passage through the dissonance of Earth's disharmony: the fear of change.

Know that your fearing these events creates far more turmoil and disruption on personal and interplanetary levels than does your acceptance of them—your understanding that the Earth Changes are the manifestation of your deity in transformation (just as they are the reflection of all life within the earth realm) and that Gaia knows exactly what to do.

The vibratory patterns of terror and fear amplify the magnitude, altering the manifestations of Earth Changes and this the Power instrumentalizes to exacerbate the emotional disharmony of your world populations.

Consider the birth process and your personal experience of that soul passing through you. Did you fear for your infant when the end of your term was upon you and you realized her painful passage from the safety of the womb was imminent?

Did you focus on the pain she would experience, attempting the seemingly impossible task of passing her mass of physical proportions through the constriction of the birth canal? Did you torment yourself with imaginings of horror and suffering?

Surely you did not. Before the splendor of (re)birth, you embraced the moment before you, putting aside even your own fear of the pain of delivering this soul into the world, and you celebrated the miracle and the beauty of life unfolding.

You opened yourself without question, trusting that all was and is forever right in the Universe, and in a second in your illusive time, an innocent and helpless new life came into your world and was placed into your awaiting arms: a soul who chose you, blessed one, to guide her into the light.

So it will be with the ascension. The Earth Mother has carried you to term. She has borne the weight and the burden of the entire human race and is now preparing to take her place on the birthing table—where all will pass to other realms and there, too, will you be embraced and cared for.

For the ascending, that will be a lighter level of consciousness, where much of the disharmony of your current lives will no longer cling and new perceptions will guide you all on your perennial journey back to Source.

… and for those who don't ascend—what will happen to these souls?

There will be another lifetime, a rebirth, once they have gone to the Halls of Learning, acquired new information regarding the next incarnation, and rested. Then they will leap back into the density of the physical reality, somewhere … sometime … as the soul decrees and designs the new experience in body and form.

How that body will take form and in what environment it will find a resonant field in which to develop is a process of karmic patterns and decisions created by the soul.

… but if Earth leaves the physical universe in ascent? What opportunity will there be for these souls to reincarnate?

We remind you that thousands of earth reflections exist in the material realm—in your infinite material universe and in equally vast parallel universes. You, yourselves, have experienced other worlds before coming into this lifetime. Indeed, many of you have that distant recall of being from another planet—from other star systems and yes, even other universes!

It is essential to your understanding of this aspect of existence that you accept and embrace the knowledge that there are countless planetary environments where living beings, often similar to you in form and nature, exist and flourish.

What can you tell us about the future of the animals and the plant world? Will they ascend as well?

In the process of light body refinement and the imminent passage through the ascension cords of your Solar Deity, the gardens of Earth will reassemble their cellular units (as will human forms) to absorb and reflect greater quanta of photons and, therefore, there will naturally be a greater translucency to their structural aspect.

The Universe is tuned to form and transmute DNA in planetary systems in harmony with the elemental energies that exist in any given environment—where life is determined to spring forward.

Consider this hypothesis:

The four elements of Earth (air, fire, water, and earth) are of themselves living entities ruled by elemental spirits, which exist in the ethereal world—a consciousness framework parallel to yours.

These have been identified by your mystics, respectively, as: sylphs, salamanders, undines, and gnomes—and all are ruled by the angelic beings, who are the High Spirits of the etheric realms. Of these:

The Air Spirits (sylphs) exist in the highest vibratory frequency of the elements that form the Earth and all bio-forms of Earth. They interact with human beings in aspects that regard the intelligent mind (impulses along the neuron pathways), the conceptualization of the Universe, thought, communication, and philosophy.

The Fire Spirits (salamanders) exist in the flame: they interact with human energy patterns, the collective passion and will, the body electric.

The Water Spirits (undines) exist within the water itself: they are directly involved with the spiritual content of the waters of Gaia and exist in the emotional body of human beings, animals, and plants.

Water is the quintessential aspect of earth consciousness, much as fire is of the planet Mars (in its present state). The Water Spirits are being called upon to assist in the restructuring of all DNA of life forms on your planet, as it is of the greatest significance to the accelerating alteration of your DNA that the cellular waters be pure and vibrating at their highest frequencies, in order to perform their function as intercellular data transmitters. They interact with the living beings of Gaia at the emotional level.

The Earth Spirits (gnomes) relate to the mineral kingdom— Spirit at a slower vibration. This realm provides the nutrients for the plant and animal kingdoms and is the foundation of all life forms on the planet.

These spirit beings will be resonating to the higher frequencies of the fourth dimension and (as complex as this may seem to you) they, too, experience altered consciousness, as the density refines to a higher frequency. This is valid for the plant families, for the animals, and for human life.

We do wish to emphasize to you that the emotional state of the animals is extremely important to the question of their ascension. Those who are abused; those who have been subjected to the cages of perpetrators of cruelty in all forms—however noble the inflictors of torture believe their work to be; those who are abandoned; those who experience the slow extermination of their species in the wild ... all those animals suffering at the hand of man will not proceed through the ascension process with you.

It is important, so important, to consider the emotional nature of the animals and their relationship to the Earth and to be loving, responsible caretakers.

Human beings, animals, plants, minerals: all interact in the process; all are experiencing the shift, at some degree or another.

What about the dolphins and the whales?

Although they appear to you as "creatures" of your seas, the Dolphin Beings and the Great Whales are not "animals" as you intend them any less than you, *Homo sapiens,* are representative of the animal kingdom.

Rather, they are highly evolved beings, whose presence on Earth has been dedicated to weaving the frequencies of the oceans, holding the balance of the waters of Gaia.

This they had accomplished with great eloquence through to the time of your second global war, despite the slaughter and destruction of so many, by the ruthless hands of the exterminators.

From that moment forward, there has been such electromagnetic and sonar interference that they have been thrown off course—and that has been a deliberate and ongoing intention of the power elite overseeing and creating much of the chaos in earth events.

In response to this abuse (and in preparation of their service to you on other planes), they have recently determined, as a group soul collective, that it is time to leave you.

We know how this disturbs you, the awakening, for your hearts are attuned to the music of the Dolphins Beings—in perfect harmony—and you have such respect and love of the Great Whales.

Take comfort in knowing that they are all ascending well in advance of the great shift ahead of you and still are working with you from the higher dimensions.

As we stated earlier, many are here with us, working members of the Sirian High Council.

That is fascinating. How do you speak to each other?

Verbal communication is a necessity at the third density in which you reside. At the next level and onward, there is no need for a common denominator of acquired language, for we communicate through telepathic waves. We are gifted with instantaneous thought transference and clarity of intent and expression, for inherent in thought transference is the lack of deception and crafted meanings.

Underlying all communication is the Highest Good of the All.

... and yet you speak to us with such eloquence!

We utilize the gifts of the receiver/transmitters, such as our channel Trydjya, who crystallize thought into the written word. We come through the hands of the attuned painter, whose brush paints the emotion into landscapes on your minds. We can be heard by the maestro, who freezes our thoughts into musical patterns that can then be read and re-created by the musicians.

All of these manifestations, we believe, speak to you. It is not the construct of language alone.

Other channeled teachings as well as some of our most important metaphysical books suggest we are moving not to the fourth dimension—but rather to the fifth. Which is correct?

The fourth dimension is a sort of clearing station between the lower and higher dimensions—similar to the human heart chakra as the clearing center for your higher chakras.

Given the intense frequencies that are tearing at Gaia, your planetary mother is not necessarily ready and evolved to the point where she has cleared all negative karma from her body, and you are, remember, the atoms, the cells, the tissues of the Mother!

In the process of passing through the ascension cord of Ra, much of this disharmony will be released, purified from the vibratory patterns of the lower energies. In the fourth dimension, more complex aspects of dualism and polarity will be refined into that which will then reflect as a more light-filled, luminous celestial body, as will be the form and essence of living beings passing with her.

Some of your species will leap even further ahead, surpassing the fourth dimension altogether. Many of the evolved souls on Earth will take quantum leaps into higher dimensions—some will even join us on this plane. Of these, some will precede you in order to assist you upon arrival.

Remembering what we have told you in the teachings, that we are **you** in the context of your future selves ... that should not be surprising to you.

What is of importance here is the entirety—the Solar Logos as it is comprised of all life, all form, all the planetary beings of Ra, all consciousness—not just individual units of life on the Great Planet Earth.

To those of you who come away from this thought wondering at which level you will find yourselves, know this: your soul has already set its course and it is your every thought, every action, and every word that lead you to your next stop on the highway of existence.

Beware not to delude yourselves with the ramblings of your wildest imagination.

It is your ability to love unconditionally, beyond ego gratification, past the concerns of your personality.

It is the heart, dear ones: the heart, the heart, the heart.

Will we have physical form in the fourth dimension?

Yes, although they will be lighter and more translucent. It is in the fifth dimension that the soul no longer creates form—from the fifth upward.

In the fourth dimension, you will be able to see through things—in every sense of the words. You will still have the experience of form, but it will not appear as dense as it currently does to you.

Know that each dimension is made up of overtones and hues. In the higher aspects of the fourth, you are in rainbow colors; in the lower, you are still confronted with the dissonant remnants of what has come through from the third. There you are still in opacity and there can be much shadow where light is beginning to weave the golden threads of liberation.

There will be healing to be done, the clearing of unharmonious thought forms, the unplugging of karmic cords, and the release from earth grids. All of this you will do in full consciousness and forgiveness, recognizing how you co-create all reality.

It is our experience that in the early stages of four-dimensional consciousness, newly arriving souls still desire the illusions of physicality, as it is experienced in the third dimension, and, hence, much energy is put into re-creating the illusion, until they acquire a greater awareness of the new. As such, we ask you to rest assured that, as you achieve initiation, four-dimensional reality will be far more familiar to you than you can imagine.

Indeed, for some—there will be no immediate recognition of the passing other than the sense that, in wakening from sleep, the world will seem so much brighter than it was the night before: so, so, so much brighter.

3

Your Evolving DNA

Humankind has reached that point in its advancing awareness of the genetic formulae of life whereby the race is now capable of altering the supreme mathematics of the Creator to reconstruct the primordial patterns of biological substance. You are relearning (or more precisely, you are **remembering**) the knowledge of the late Atlanteans, handed down to countless societies over the score of human experience, with which you are capable of designing and restructuring beings of all proportions—from the minutiae of molecular units to the biological complexity of your own species or that of alien seed—into new hybrid forms and mutations.

The Maya, the Egyptians, and countless other civilizations of your written and unwritten history have accessed this information, as you are now. In essence, you are experiencing and bringing into the foreground of human knowledge that godly wisdom with which Creation formulates, constructs, and then builds even further upon the cosmometry of its own design.

Most progressive civilizations eventually reach this stage in their evolution, for, as gods in their own right, all intelligent members of those societies that traverse the furthest corners of the material universe are ultimately compelled to rediscover the secrets of their individual existence, as well as the workings of the greater whole—the Cosmos of Soul.

Unfortunately, the magnificence of such potential in the hands of the human race is being diminished by materialistic man's arrogant denial of Spirit and aborted through his irreverent application of genetic technology—some of which you are being sold to believe serves for the survival and advancement of your race ... and much of which is being utilized in secret by the designers of covert technologies, biological warfare and humanoid-robotics, soon to appear amongst you.

Where there is balance, a reverence for the perfection of the Divine Plan prevents the destructive force from taking that most important of discoveries to its dark vibration—where grotesque manipulation of the genetic codes embedded in the DNA upsets the harmonies of the living and lowers the celestial vibrations of universal mind. Where there is not (as is the case in your own evolutionary schematic as primary residents of Earth), untold disruption in planetary harmonics sound the discord through every level and every resonant realm.

This you are witnessing now, as your journey through the Desert Days takes you to the fringes of sanity, and where the blatant destruction of the splendid Garden of Eden burns your imprint upon the immortal soul of Gaia.

Well you can imagine how thin is the grey line between "being" gods, co-creators of the Universe, and "playing" God with the principles of Creation. Indeed, that fine distinction is surely a most profound philosophical thread upon which great debate and theosophical considerations may be duly based—one with which you may sew new "empirical clothes" for your contemporary societies.

Our Elders and their team of genetic technicians learned how very fine that line of distinction was, and the implications of having crossed it, from the karma they created for Sirius and other alien worlds, for the results of the Great Experiment that unfolded on Earth wove our lowered vibration into the karmic designs and soul patterns of the starseeded human race.

Whereas those of the higher dimensions (the Alliance formed of Angel Warriors, the Andromeda Network, Ascended Masters, luminaries from the seventh, eighth, and ninth dimensions, Sirian Elders, and Pleiadian Light Emissaries) were toning light frequencies into the crystalline waters of your DNA matrix, the others, such as the Engan, were primarily committed to the biochemical aspects of your seed—the genetic drivers of their race— for it was the survival of their species that was their focus.

However their genetic imprint would be modified in the New World, their species would live on in the starseed generations.

It was their need to escape extinction, a truly three-dimensional perspective, that was their intention from the start and that was indeed a necessary element for the seeding. Unfortunately, that fear-based consciousness (the polar aspect of the positive survival consciousness you needed to flourish in the wilds of the Earth) was also imprinted within you from the beginning.

When the grid was placed around you, de-activating ten light-coded strands of DNA, the fundamental weaknesses of all four master strains became far more prominent aspects of the human experience. From that moment on, you became entangled in a struggle between the lower and higher vibrations of your genetic "memory," and then de-activated by the base frequencies of Annunaki electromagnetic fields.

Stunned, you were trapped, so soon after your incubation, in their powerful nets—and there you have remained, until now, when (despite their desperate attempts to reweave it) the net is disintegrating in the brilliance that pours forth from the ascending soul essence of Ra.

No More Secrets, No More Lies

The teachings describe our being limited to two strands of DNA, as a reflection of our being locked into extreme polarity on this planet. Please explain this concept in greater detail.

The essential elements of your DNA are formed of the most minute vibrational waves of spiraling light from your Sun, which serve as pathways upon which subatomic particles of all biological forms are attracted into spiraling light filaments of consciousness.

One single strand of DNA is one of these light filaments: it is a long polynucleotide chain, which, in a healthy biological environment, extends the full length of a chromosome.

Double-stranded DNA, with which you have been operating for over one hundred thousand years, contains two such chains, held together by precise hydrogen bonding between nitrogenous bases. In this arrangement, each base of one strand is bonded to its complementary base at the same level in the other strand, forming specific base pairs, which stretch from one backbone to the other.

Geometric constraints imposed by this double helix, in which the two strands of DNA twist around a cosmometrically perfect dyad axis, dictate that the strands run in opposite directions. This means the two strands are of opposite polarity, a sort of mirror to each other, and this defines your reality in the universe of matter—where polar forces exist as opposites of each other.

As you integrate and crystallize the third strand of DNA, which will bond with the other two via the same biochemical process of hydrogen bonding, you will be creating triangulation in the DNA. As you are aware, the triangle is the first form of your Euclidean geometry and, vibrationally, it represents the resolution of the perennial battle for balance in the polarity of two.

Numerous people and websites currently offer guidance regarding the activation of twelve, twenty-two, one hundred and forty-four ... even thousands of strands of DNA—in workshops or even by means of remote activation over the telephone! Please explain why you are focused on the importance of activating only one more strand and how it can be successfully achieved.

We invite you to be as discerning as possible before the many exorbitant claims that are being placed before you, at this time of rapid acceleration and the creation of new paradigms for human evolution. Ask yourself if your ego is being activated by the information and the claims that are being made by the designers of the information highways.

As two-stranded beings (in heart-centered consciousness), you are magnificent. You are capable of infinite creativity; you have the capacity for genius of intellect; you can reach the vibrational frequencies of untold beauty and light; and, most importantly, you are reservoirs of immeasurable love and selflessness.

However, the information that will be woven into your intelligence codex with the third strand of DNA accomplishes the most significant, perhaps, of all your leaps in awareness: it creates triangulation in the DNA, reconstructing the fundamental blueprint upon which you will reconnect the galactic heritage that has eluded you.

We believe this to be the most significant aspect of your awakening: remembering who you are and where you have come from, remembering your stellar heritage. In this process, you repair the miasmas in the astral/causal bodies and reweave the cosmometry of illuminated conscience.

In our experience and observation, no human being on Earth at this time has reached twelve-stranded awareness and we cannot, from our perspective, confirm claims such as those you have referred.

It is our understanding and experience that the ascending will acquire full twelve-stranded consciousness at the time of passing. At your density in the current phase of your planet, twelve strands of DNA light filaments would blow all your circuitry and blast you right out of your bodies—not unlike plugging directly into a lightning storm at full raging force.

As for the process of integrating the third strand, we have provided relevant information to you in our material and, for some of you, it is available through direct interaction with our channel, who links you to us in the process.

The very nature of earth acceleration and the rapidly disintegrating electromagnetic net of dark design are creating the vibrational tenor in which the third strand of DNA can find the proper harmonics for reassembly and integration.

You can accelerate the process now, facilitating heightened awareness at this time of awesome change—a quickening—or you can continue to do your spiritual questing, awaiting the moment when this activation occurs, spontaneously, within you.

However rapidly you wish to leap into the realms of the awakened ... however frustrated you are at the process you must go through at this time of upheaval ... know that leap you will, as awakening twenty-first-century beings of Gaia.

It is your birthright, starseed.

A new day dawns.

Can you clarify just how this third strand of DNA will be activated?

You can accelerate the integration of the third strand and the subsequent activation of the pineal gland by imprinting (intentionally and with great focused intent) the higher octave harmonics and the cosmometry of your evolving consciousness within the cellular waters of your body.

In so doing, you lay down the blueprint upon which the activated strands of DNA, formed of the tiniest spiraling waves of the Sun's light, gather the subatomic particles of Gaian energy into spiraling light filaments of consciousness.

The activation is a term we use to describe the magnetization of the essential elements of dormant DNA, now lying scattered within your genetic markers, into the light strands of etheric memory, to be woven into a superconducting tetrahedral thread of consciousness that weaves in the memory of your starseed.

Will this third strand of DNA manifest itself as a physical aspect of our genetic makeup and, if so, shouldn't it be identifiable at this point by the scientific community?

All the genetic material of your twelve-stranded consciousness lies within your physical being—scrambled—awaiting reassembly. This information is of the utmost importance to your deciphering the mysteries of your struggle and your way out of limitation.

Your scientists are well aware that these bits of the puzzle, those mysterious snippets of noncoding DNA within the chromosomes or genomes, are far more than "junk," which until only recently were believed to serve no purpose, in what is otherwise a most miraculous, perfect design of life in biological form.

There are incredible discoveries currently breaking in the geneticists' laboratories. At this time of emerging knowledge and the shifting awareness of *Homo sapiens,* these and other proofs are about to be revealed and yet, only those of you who understand the significance of these mutations will grasp the magnitude of such revelations.

Know that trained psychics are currently working with the scientists to identify the etheric energy lines, upon which the snippets of genetic material are reorganizing into the complex formations of higher octave DNA. When these bits of information weave together, the vibrational frequency of the formation will be off the charts, so to speak, of the viewers ... but soon, very soon now, they will see.

What matters most is that you feel the explosion within you and, moreover, that you focus not upon the phenomena of your personal evolution but upon your mission as the awakening of Gaia.

It is pretty difficult to embrace the idea that this monumental transformation, the acquisition of additional strands of DNA, is now occurring in our species. How can there be additional strands of DNA that science has not identified?

Science at the onset of the twenty-first century on Earth has made a gargantuan leap in the decoding of human genetics: the teams have only broken a fraction of the complex codex of genetic blueprints of all living beings on your planet. This comes with great possibilities as well as an enormous responsibility.

Misused, unfortunately, it has already resulted in dire consequences for the human race and for the animals and plants gracing Earth at this pivotal time in your galactic transformation.

From cells in the petri dish to wild hybrids in laboratory cages, genetically mutated bio-forms have either already appeared in your plant and animal kingdoms or they are soon to be unleashed upon you. This aspect of DNA reorganization the geneticists seem to be mastering well, if "well" it can be described.

No doubt you intuit that we believe little good can come of such experimentation, considering the consciousness behind such manipulations.

Ironically, the establishment continues to adhere to the simplistic and utterly inadequate explanation of complex human genetics being comprised of eighty percent pure "junk" within you: eighty percent junk! We wish to suggest that had the scientific communities of Earth been funded to pursue the study of human DNA for the highest purpose with the same intensity as they have been to toy with genetic manipulation for commercial and military uses, they would surely know, by now, how to reassemble the scattered bits and pieces for full light body consciousness.

Yes, but then … your awakening to the legacy of your seed, full light body awareness, is the last thing the Power desires, as they desperately seek to bring Gaia down into the darkness of their Nebiruan doom.

Neither do they understand nor are they funded to explore your multidimensional, extraterrestrial seeds and origins and therefore they dismiss as sheer lunacy the possibility that what they have denied and deemed "junk" within every human being is anything but that. They refuse to even consider that the scattered material within you has a most incredible purpose and that is coming to light now.

You, the awakening, are realizing and remembering that you hold within you an additional ten strands of DNA (your multidimensional, galactic linkage)—dormant, awaiting activation.

The science to which you refer has, to date, identified and decoded the physical manifestation of twenty percent of the DNA codex of *Homo sapiens:* its biochemical, electromagnetic composition. They are still in the dark, so to speak, as to the meaning of the eighty percent they are unable to identify.

Do you realize the incredible bluff that has been perpetrated upon the human race? Science claims absolute authority over Truth and yet it gets away with perpetuating the idea that eighty percent of your makeup is "junk"?

As we understand junk to be "waste" and unnecessary to any

system, we have great difficulty in understanding how this concept has been embraced as Truth and why the minds of human beings have not questioned such a blanket of ignorance as to their own existence.

We are encouraged to see that you are finally recognizing how much more there is to the story of human genetics. The "time" of self-discovery of the entire race is upon you.

As Earth accelerates her electromagnetic fields in preparation for ascension, all living beings in her embrace are also accelerating and these waves of intense energy are disintegrating the grid, which caused these bits of bioelectrical data to scatter from the onset of your species.

These enormous waves of cosmic energy are magnetizing the snippets of DNA into their etheric structures, to be reorganized into the complex weaving of the multidimensional sacred geometries that will define your existence in light body.

You state that we will acquire the full twelve-stranded consciousness at the time of our passing into the higher dimension. Isn't that Christ Consciousness and, if so, isn't it unreasonable to think that from our current state we will leap to the light of an ascended master?

This question is filled with complexity. It is, however, a brilliant one. We will attempt to simplify it into a framework you can accept at this time.

Masters of the Universe, such as the Christed One, are capable of communicating heart light at such an unfathomable spectrum of vibrations that they are simultaneously present and fully capable of participating at every corner of space, time, and in the infinite wisdom of light everlasting.

Masters of such brilliance carry the intelligence codes of the spiral of light itself; they **are** the spiral upon which we journey— the template.

The DNA wiring of your biological being evolves into a luminous circuit board through which you will plug your consciousness into the Gossamer Web, the light grid of the Cosmos, as you proceed through your experience.

In a not too distant future (as we intend time to mean your evolution to higher frequency) you will no longer identify your "I am" presence as separate from any other light being in the multidimensional Universe.

As a twelve-stranded Avatar, you will have decoded the mystery of it all and recognized that the entire physical universe is merely a holographic projection of infinitely and brilliantly connected DNA light codings, which traverse the Cosmos.

If, indeed, it is our future to experience twelve strands of DNA as ascending light beings, why do you deem it so important to undertake the process of accelerating it now?

As Gaia fine-tunes her etheric and physical bodies in preparation for passage, all living beings on the planet are undergoing increasingly extreme energy shifts in their auric fields—manifesting, for some, as incredible emotional imbalance, physical discomfort, and fear-inducing survival issues.

By consciously undergoing the process of activating the dormant, detached light strands of DNA, you are aligning your consciousness with that higher frequency to which the Earth is beginning to resonate. You are setting the intention that it be so. This conscious effort and your focused intent have an enormous effect on releasing those energy blocks and reestablishing the harmony and joy with which you will look to your future—a legacy that will soon be manifest as the "right now" of your experience.

We wish to reiterate that, of the gross and subtle accelerations you are experiencing at this time, none will be as important to your process as the integration of the third strand of DNA—which, activated, weaves itself into the polarized double-helix chemical strand, creating triangulation: the cosmometric blueprint for the assimilation of the additional light codes.

I'm having enormous difficulty assimilating the concept of DNA and its relationship to our current electromagnetic form and the existence of this form in the multidimensional Universe. Can you explain the interaction between our current DNA formation and the significance of the morphogenetic field?

The soul focuses its intention to create a template, body, physical vehicle—to exist in a three-dimensional context. It seeks resonance within a morphogenetic field, wherein it can manifest its desire to experience the density of 3D and then builds the biochemical template from the collective DNA imprint for that particular species and the environment in which it has decided to create form.

So are you suggesting, then, that the accelerating DNA is actually manifest as physical form and, if so, shouldn't we be able to identify it in those who have already activated?

DNA activation (as we intend it) involves the establishment of the proper harmonics within the electromagnetic human form, whereby the etheric imprint of the crucial third strand of DNA is reconstructed from the dormant genetic materials that lie within you, awaiting organization. The snippets of scattered genetic material (that which your scientists refer to as "junk" within you) become magnetically attracted to the light gatherer, the etheric strand, and eventually take form. This form has already been observed in laboratories and soon this information will be shared with you.

Is it the same with animals as with humans—consciously creating their physical beings—and are they, too, experiencing the metamorphosis of their DNA?

Absolutely. How else do you think they come to be the intuitive, intelligent beings that they are? Look into the eyes of your loving canine, the curious feline. Do you not see the conscious soul looking back at you? Observe birds as they organize, their communities, their eloquence of song, their sensitivity to Gaia's magnetic currents—is theirs not a profound consciousness?

The distinct difference between their process and that of humankind is that they were never wired, as you, to hold twelve-stranded Christ Consciousness on Earth.

What about the plants and the trees?

The question of the flora of Earth differs in that the consciousness of plants is collective to the genus and species of each variety. All the plants and tree communities of your world create complex energy grids upon the land and seas of Gaia, as emotional sentinels of the Earth Mother. They are far more emotional than you have ever understood. They exist in your world to bring beauty, many layers of healing, and nourishment to the biosphere.

Mass destruction of the plant families and the tall trees of your once pristine forests, caused primarily by human hand, has everything to do with the enormous imbalance in the Earth and in human emotional patterns across the planet.

You have much to learn with regard to the relationship between the flora of Gaia and your own emotional equilibrium.

Alteration of their DNA in genetically modified food experiments is altering the emotional state of the oceans, the forests (or what remains of them), and the valleys of Gaia. The global destruction of the flora and the deliberate mutation of the molecular structure—DNA modification—naturally has a direct affect on the animals, the human race, the atmosphere, and the energy lines of the entire planetary body.

I have read about Dr. Emoto's work regarding conscious water and the study of the crystalline nature of water. Can you elaborate more as to the significance of water with regard to the activation of our DNA?

The process of DNA activation involves a higher dimensional sacred geometry coming into form within your biological structures at the cellular level.

Your body is primarily water and it is the communication network of all consciousness as it passes from cell to cell through the blood.

The scientists have been able to show you the hexagonal nature of water crystals and you have been introduced to the effect of conscious thought upon form through the successful photography of exquisite water crystals.

However, with the acquisition of new codes coming through in the Language of Light, the waters of your being are becoming imprinted with hyperdimensional blueprints that will awaken and restructure the scattered light filaments lying dormant within you. This is a higher form of order and design than the hexagonal water crystals that you see in those images—it is the sacred geometry of your evolution into light beings.

It is important to understand how the cosmometry of light flowing into your beings at this time in your personal and planetary evolution carries an inscription of the higher vibration that is translated into geometric codes and transmitted through the cells of your being—into the DNA—via your cellular bio-water.

As you begin to activate the light codes of your accelerating DNA, the complex biochemical changes taking place in the biosphere of your physical bodies are being communicated, via the cellular waters, through the neural transmitters, activating the hypothalamus—the pineal gland.

4

Imminent Contact

The Councils of many alien nations have convened and are moving in, despite the barriers being fortified in earth space. The governments simply cannot prevent you from receiving open contact with representatives of pioneering extraterrestrial civilizations, no matter how they intensify the smoke screen.

Contact is imminent.

You know it is—you realize that the Secret Government cannot keep the evidence from you any longer. You know that the sightings are proliferating everywhere around the world and that even the mainstream media, however silenced to truth, can no longer avoid the unavoidable. People everywhere on Earth have begun to take notice of new lights in the heavens—lights that dance, lights that move about, lights that illuminate the undeniable fact that humankind's isolation is coming to a most exciting end.

Despite the Power's desperate efforts (for desperate they are indeed) to conceal all they know of the alien life that thrives beyond and within your parameters, there is simply no way to prevent your discovery of the hidden domains. Contact is soon to be made with the people of Planet Earth—in your lifetimes. You are all going to experience this, no matter where you stand on the question of human evolution and the coming Earth Changes.

Meanwhile, the power elite continue to bombard the collective unconscious with fearful and utterly frightening images of alien archetypes (and plenty do they know of dark beings, near and far!) in order to hold your wandering minds at bay. Rather than having you roam the Universe, fascinated by the glorious potential of your membership in the Galactic Federation of Worlds, they much prefer you lock your vivid imaginations into the terrifying possibilities of an alien "invasion" of body-snatching creatures, who wish to strip you of your sovereignty and control your bodies, minds, and souls.

How "curiously" ironic that they should see alien activity on Earth in that way, isn't it?

No More Secrets, No More Lies

You have alluded to our imminent contact with extraterrestrials, but have not committed to the actual timing of this global event. Can you also be more specific as to what alien beings are actually intervening or interacting with human beings?

At this moment, there are the Annunaki hybrids, who run your global corporations and they, in turn, run your governments, described at length in our works regarding the power elite. There are the Zeta Reticulans, at work in your military and scientific control centers. There are alien colonies underwater, in your oceans and under the Earth's surface layer, managing a complex network of subterranean colonies and breeding centers, aquaculture farms, experimental laboratories, weapons and energy storage centers. There are the Alpha Draconians, reptilian in nature, feeding off the lower vibrations of your species.

There are countless others at work there on Earth for the completion of their own agendas. Alien species of every form and level of intelligence cover your planet: amoebae with telepathic capacities capable of testing and surviving in any geophysical environment currently exist on your planet; creatures of the seas are being utilized by alien colonists as transporters and energy sources; alien microbes, bacteria, thought forms, genetically created creatures of every possible invention also abound.

You have alien beings with relatively perfect human form in your governments, your corporations, your communications organizations and they are unrecognizable to you because they appear to be exactly like you—until you look deeply into their eyes.

When you gaze deeply into the eyes of an alien you know that it is not your species looking back. You always know, whether or not you are capable of identifying just what it is that is not familiar to you.

This is why they rarely look you in the eye.

You have communication from extra-dimensional intelligence coming in from the light realms of the fifth dimension onwards, involving Pleiadian, Sirian, Arcturian, and Andromedan light beings assisting earth beings and those of your sister planets, with much attention being focused on the celestial Venus, Mars, Jupiter, and Saturn in primary focus.

You have uninterrupted visitation from alien craft and projections of them in your night skies (although the masses are seeing, but not believing) from the most barren outposts of your planet to those locations of greatest population density.

You have crop circles, radio transmissions, and signs of contact everywhere around you.

Therefore, to say that you will have contact "in the future" is somewhat misrepresentative of the extraterrestrial reality as it pertains to alien species' presence upon and intervention with your Earth.

However, what we intend as "irrefutable proof of contact" will take place at that point in your passage when you are in the "between": when you are detaching from the third dimension and a breath away from moving through the astral cord of Ra.

This time begins with the completion of your year 2012.

You enter the docking stage at that time.

What do you mean by the "docking stage"?

We intend that to mean the time of the final alignments before your passing through the ascension cord, as determined by the tuning of all celestial beings just before the great symphony of Ra.

Of the alien race or races that are about to make global contact with Earth, can you please tell us where specifically they will be from and what will their purpose be?

The alien intelligence that will organize the massive global contact that will catapult human consciousness will be representatives of the Galactic Federation and they will be concerned with assuring that no direct intervention from outside alien forces (and those already present on Earth) be allowed to create a global Armageddon on your planet and nearby space.

They will serve as the models upon which you will first face and then deal with the alien reality.

They will ensure that the universal laws of noninterventionism and peaceful co-existence between worlds be the vision with which the ascending of Earth prepares to co-create the four-dimensional collective.

Consider, too, how humankind is moving about in space (for your probes and ships are reaching far out into the solar system) and know that you are being perceived in the same way—as aliens—to beings on neighboring planets with whom you have identified yourselves and are already communicating.

... but isn't their appearing to us, of itself, a form of intervention?

We understand interventionism to mean any attempt to alter and disrupt or direct the course of a sovereign being, state, or environment for the self-fulfilling purposes that are determined by the intervening force.

With regard to the complex question of planets, such as yours, that have devolved to the point that they are nearing the point of self-annihilation and possibly the destruction of other celestial domains, then it is a different matter.

It becomes a matter of serving the greater good.

Earth is being managed by secretive forces that are in alliance with extraterrestrial races, which have secret agendas for the future of the planet and its sentient species ... and this can no longer be allowed to continue nor to escalate further.

Add to this situation the imminent passage of your planet and the greater family of planetary bodies and communities and you can understand why it is necessary to provide you with the interplanetary model of civilized worlds and the Brother/Sisterhood of conscious beings in the Universe.

By presenting you with the model, all are intent upon helping you create the reality from your conscious awareness and that, it is determined, is assistance—but not intervention.

What about the Greys? What is their purpose in the overall alien plan for the human race?

Greys are neither of the physical nor the spiritual realms—they are a species that somehow resides in a sort of plasma vortex—hovering somewhere between life and death, existence and nonexistence, darkness and light. This we have described to you as the "grey zone."

Over the last fifty of your earth years, they have managed to project themselves into the mass mind of *Homo sapiens*—first in delta wave dream states, then in alpha waking states. In so doing, they reach resonance with you to the point that they can achieve the vibration necessary to materialize form on the physical plane for very brief periods of time.

In essence, they are occasionally pulled out of the grey zone and into your reality because they ride in on the resonant mind waves that have been created in the collective human consciousness.

In most actual cases of human encounter with Greys, the mind of the human contactee is frozen in a state of mind-controlled paralysis, while they, the experimenters, proceed with their collection of sperm or ova to be used in laboratories later on.

It is very similar to the way some insect species inject their prey with paralyzing venom before their subjects are ingested.

In the case of their human subjects, however, there actually is no intention to destroy or harm. Theirs is merely a clinical exercise in which you, the subjects, are viewed as the genetically superior animal species of the earth biosphere and it is because of that genetic superiority that they are intent upon collecting and cataloging first, human DNA material and, second, that of select animal species.

Attempts to create a hybrid alien/human form, for the time being, have failed, but they are attempting to find the answers that will facilitate the survival of their own endangered species. You can see it repeated time and time again. In the end, you understand, the driving forces of life in the Universe are survival and procreation of the species.

Your scientists treat animals in the same way, often with far less humanity than the Greys use upon their human contacts. We wonder why those abuses do not disturb human thoughts or why parallels are hardly ever drawn.

Those of you who understand the laws of karma recognize how your abuse of the animals and your manipulations of genetic information draw this alien abuse upon the human race as a whole.

The Greys have been particularly active on Earth in the last fifty years of your time and have managed to successfully collect and classify a vast library and bank of human genetic codes.

Intent upon redirecting their evolution into a race of hybrid Grey-humanoid species that would be biological in nature in order to anchor in the 3D realm, their ambition is not unlike your mad scientists' fascination with creating a biological robot that eventually requires no physical form—only in reverse!

Surely you must see the irony in the idea that there are alien species attempting to reconstruct their biological presence from a purely mental, semi-etheric nature, while the techno-maniacs of the human realm are burning with the desire to discard their human forms to take residence within a computer ... in order to relocate their conscious minds somewhere in hyperspace!

Whether you make the correlation between the illusion of your dimension and the fabrication of artificial space—hyperspace— is a subject for far lengthier debate amongst you, as you question more and more the true nature of existence.

So are you saying that contact and abduction until now have been based on this purpose: the creation of a hybrid race?

We are stating that of the abduction reports from hundreds of thousands of individuals in your populations worldwide, most have been dealing with Grey technicians and that the purpose of their abductions of human beings is to catalog and store human genetic and reproductive material to be used in creating a new species—yes.

However, we ask you always to bear in mind that many of the abduction scenarios described by victimized human beings are, in actuality, your own government secret operatives taking citizens for their own agendas. They operate under the guise of extraterrestrials, because it is an excellent cover and it dismisses the contactee as a fraud or a victim of his/her own delusions.

Why would the Secret Government go to such great lengths to conduct these abductions and yet cover them up to the mainstream?

If you begin with the precept that the Secret Government is actually run by alien Annunaki and their hybrid offspring—you should be able to reach your own conclusions.

You are being lied to, misled, and misdirected with the intent of frightening you into submission, while the Power sets up a scenario that you are helpless before a future of alien contact.

Inherent in their design, you understand, is the fear-based, controlling paradigm that manipulates the population into believing that only they, your leaders, can save you from the ultimate "terrorists": your perennial nemesis.

Clearly, your growing awareness that the very ones who would position themselves as your saviors from alien invaders are themselves aliens creates a wildly fantastic story-line that few can imagine and to which even fewer would dare speak.

However, we know you know better.

We know you can see beyond.

If you are reading these messages it is because you have the vision to see past the camouflage that is being created for you and we are committed to helping as many of you as we possibly can to see beyond the secrets and lies and to awaken to new horizons for the soul of humanity.

We are committed to helping you to embrace this moment, rather than to fear it and we have found the channel who dares to speak of such realities.

She, in turn, has found you—who dare to listen.

What effect will their arrival—the contact moment—have upon the human race?

Ask yourself what it will mean to the human race to finally have undeniable, unquestionable proof of alien visitation: validation that the Universe is filled with intelligent, communicating civilizations dedicated to the exploration of life throughout the galaxy and to peaceful co-existence within that shared level of reality.

Despite your media machines' depictions of the most nightmarish alien caricatures, you hope and dream of an interplanetary community—the *Star Trek* archetype.

Imagine how your world populations will react to finally being contacted by intelligent, peaceful beings whose purpose in coming to you is to welcome you into a galactic community, where intercultural exchange and communication between worlds are the goal and the reality.

No longer will you be limited to conjecture, secret agendas, doubt, or denial: no longer will the Power hold the knowledge in their hands.

Alien races, many strikingly similar to yours, will stand before you, en masse, at the appointed hour.

Rest assured you will be utterly amazed to find that in so many ways you will feel you are looking into a mirror, seeing your own reflection—perhaps your future selves—shining back to you.

What will it mean to know that all the petty wars now destroying your world have been distracting you from ever believing that there can be harmony between "different" races, religions, and countries—all that separates you from the other?

War on Earth, with all its profiteering and senseless violence, will cease.

What will it mean to you to be released, finally, from the orphanage of your isolation and take your rightful place in the galactic family? Hatred will be replaced with wonder and a most resounding sense of communion.

What effect will this have on the entire human race—when you finally recognize the Truth to the undying question of life beyond your tiny station in the Cosmos of Soul?

That is a question only you and the other six and one-half billion individuals on your planet can answer for each and for the entirety ... and answer it you will in the days that lie before your passage.

We, however, believe that the hardened shell of denial that encases the mass of human consciousness will crack wide open, and from that impenetrable carapace of fear and ignorance will emerge, at long last, Galactic *Homo sapiens*.

To learn that the Universe is filled with civilizations of beings, many of which are populated by almost exact replicas of human form and genetic structure, will be, of itself, the ascension of spirit and soul.

Will some of us be selected to train formally with these civilizations?

You, the awakening, are training yourselves, selecting yourselves, remembering yourselves and your missions. As you accelerate, all you have acquired in what you still understand as "past lives" and all that you will call upon from that aspect that you would think of as a "future self" are at your disposal.

There are many systems available to you now for healing, spiritual enlightenment, activation and you are the ones who are finding your way to the information and method that most resonate with your soul purpose and your vision.

There is no selection process—no elite, no chosen ones, none of this.

There is only the pure white light of your higher consciousness walking you through the labyrinth, as it twists and turns and taunts you to find the way out of illusion: out of the darkness and into the light.

5

Earth Changes and Personal Evolution

A contemporary understanding of personal evolution—your acceleration into fully conscious twenty-first-century human beings—requires profound introspection, commitment, and integration of the logical and intuitive halves of the mind. It entails a clearing of old programming, release of blocked energy forms, and a new approach to living as caretakers of the celestial being upon whom you reside and take nourishment. Involved is the full awakening of the heart and the silencing of the ego-driven self.

These are the fundamental processes that will determine how you will approach the process of planetary transformation, while defining your personal experience of ascension from the realm of matter.

As you move ever closer to the fated date of the closing Mayan calendar (December 21, 2012), you are becoming increasingly alarmed over the prospect of an impending global disaster—the Armageddon scenario—which has been rendered a highly possible reality through senseless nuclear proliferation, your poisonous waste, and your rage.

Indeed, manifestations of upheaval have already begun at every corner of the world.

Perhaps, many fear, it is too late ... and you are careening towards the inevitable, with no way to break your fall. Others understand how you create your realities with every thought, every word and gesture ... that it can be a smooth ride if you focus upon "right action"—your minds centered, clear, and filled with wonder over your potential as the New Aquarians of Planet Earth.

It is at the same time frightening, yet exciting, for you know, on some intuitional level, that you have experienced this before. Humanity obviously survived. As reincarnating beings, you have known death and rebirth over and over again, although most of you do not consciously remember your passage in and out of the physical realm. But this is quite different.

Those who have opted to be born into this earth era are experiencing the death, or transmutation, of the entire planet, and you are in the thick of it, holding on for dear life, your happiness and security constantly threatened by the specter of total annihilation.

Like the people of late Atlantis, you seem to be on the brink, anticipating your plunge into the abyss. Your concept of life and of your purpose as human beings is changing; your fragility and impermanence are ever more present in your minds; your greater home, the very earth beneath your feet, is in "clear and present" danger.

It is a difficult but challenging time and, therefore, you would do well to remember, no matter how your personal circumstances may otherwise appear, that you have chosen to be here.

Although it may seem incomprehensible to you at the conscious level, you do know about planetary evolution ... the transmutation of form and biological systems. Humanity has experienced it before, when the great antediluvian civilization of Atlantis reached such a state of disharmony that it short-circuited the energy networks of the planet, and life was nearly obliterated at many corners of the Earth.

The power structure of the time (the omnipotent forces of the Dark Priesthood of Atlán) believed, in their blind arrogance, that they could own even the forces of Gaia, harnessing her like a beast of burden. They pushed beyond the limits, and all was virtually washed away in the Great Flood, as Gaia cleansed her body of the intense negative vibration and brought herself back to center to start again, renewed and revitalized.

Here you are, once again, setting the Goddess off course, throwing everything out of balance in your exacerbation of the duality that underlies three-dimensional reality. From your limited vantage point, it appears that the very nature of existence is based on the war between good and evil and even now, as you spiral into the future, you are faced with this dualism at every juncture ... in every moment of your lives. You may have resigned yourselves to the idea that there is no hope for humanity—that you have reached the point of no return—and that is a dangerous, self-defeating belief structure. It only feeds the darkness, empowering those who believe they own you to take more from you. It amplifies the darkness, catapulting you even further into despair. It takes your light ... your power ... your joy.

You live in a world which hosts both extremely dark characters and wondrously loving, spiritual beings, but the truth is that most of humanity is somewhere in between. Each of you knows and has confronted the brilliance as well as the shadow of your own persona, and that is the duality—the very nature of life as you know it in the human experience. There have been moments of incredible radiance and impenetrable darkness throughout history and these two extremes, you find, often exist in the same moment, occupying the same space as poles of the one energy. The poles clash and conflict with each other and yet, you realize, they are simply reflections of the whole.

As students of esoteric wisdom, you are learning that you must integrate the polar aspects: the good and bad; the light and dark; the love and hate. As long as you continue to fuel these forces in opposition, there will be war on every level.

Now, more than ever, the fighting and conflagrations surround you, and humanity seems lost in the senselessness of violence and despair. It is a time of extremes in behavior, when these aspects have, once again, come into absolute conflict. Human suffering, the disregard for life and beauty, and the abuse of those who seek power over others are fast becoming the overriding experience of your contemporary civilization, causing you to question just how far it is that the human race has actually come in its course of social evolution.

You are reliving, at this time in history, the same undercurrents, energy manipulation, and abuse of power that exemplified the last generations of Atlantis ... a civilization that had reached (in some aspects) a much higher level of technological prowess than that which you know today. It was a society that enjoyed direct assistance from multidimensional beings who trained and worked with the Priesthood (themselves descendants of other realms). Their enhanced capabilities and understanding of the universal laws and elemental forces qualified them as Keepers of the Records.

These gifts of extraterrestrial knowledge were intended to raise the consciousness of your ancestors, bringing them a sense of their part in the greater scheme of things. Paradoxically, the priestesses of the early generations used the Wisdom for the light while, goaded by the Annunaki, later generations of the Priesthood saw some of the Brotherhood swing to the dark side, turning their acquired knowledge—their gifts—against the people. How can you help but notice that the time of darkness, the flagrant abuse of the Wisdom, is happening again?

We, Speakers of the Sirian High Council, confirm that many of the sophisticated technologies resulting from that exchange are being utilized against humanity and against Gaia. In their all-consuming pursuit of power, the dark priests of Atlán, united with others of Annunaki lineage, have reincarnated now. We assure you that they are more ravenous than ever in their hunger to harvest and consume your energy, your power, and your resources. Could it be that you are going to have to relive the fall of Atlantis all over again?

It is a devastating alliance, that of the dark force, yet the light is all around you. You have only to set your intention, your group mind, to penetrate and disarm the perpetrators of ignorance. Know that, no matter how determined others might be to draw upon your power, darkness can only feed on darkness and that, we remind you, is nothing more than your fear, your ignorance, and your rage. By remembering the structural nature of the dark pole, you can move through the coming Earth Changes without suffering and pain. It is your choice to make ... it always has been.

You can still alter the outcome so that, this time, the manipulation of energy and the abuse of power occurring in your realm will not have to result in the devastation that once before erased almost all life from the Great Planet Earth. You can choose not to suffer in any way whatsoever the coming transformation; rather, you can anticipate with eagerness the process of rebirthing your planet, honoring your soul's intention to take part in that experience.

Atlantis Rising

I am an oceanographer and I spend most of my life studying the life of the seas, so I was deeply fascinated by your teachings regarding the crystalline nature of water.

I am most concerned about the oceans with regard to the ecological imbalance of our planet, as I see firsthand how grave the situation truly is.

Can you give us more guidance, specifically, about healing the waters of the Earth?

We feel your deep and growing concern for the living beings of the seas and all that is pure crystalline majesty in the waters of Earth. These waves of emotion pass through us and we empathize with you and all Earth Keepers, yet we remind you that all the ecosystems of Earth are reflections or manifestations of the greater being—the mental, physical, emotional, and spiritual bodies of Gaia. We ask that you always bear that holistic concept in mind when you study her emotional body—the waters—in a somehow "separate" context.

We suggest that you cannot resolve the imbalances that are reflected back to your race from the element of water unless you are prepared to consider how the earth, air, fire, and waters all interplay in the dynamics of Gaian resonance. Never lose sight of the fact that all is interconnected.

As a guardian of the living libraries of the oceans, you know the significance of the waters of Gaia and how their vibratory essence is the determining aspect of the life that flourishes there. Deep within you, your love of the water reflects your emotional appreciation of the planetary being—your keen sensitivity to the expression of joy, rage, the peace, and the disharmony of the Goddess.

The waters constitute the emotional body of Gaia. If they are to be healed and brought back into balance, it must be done at the emotional level, through your love and respect, through your race consciousness. There must be enormous numbers of you working towards this goal—intent upon cleansing the emotional debris from the greater body of Gaia.

This has not been accomplished. The waters have been utilized as a repository for your waste. It all eventually filters into the water, every bit ... every wave. Everything washes "out to sea."

It is the playground of the distracted, the killing field of the unmerciful hunters. It has absorbed the radiation, the toxins, and high levels of estrogens (produced by much of your waste products), thus altering the living balance within it.

We believe you need to investigate the estrogen explosion within the waters. It is affecting the very nature of human reproduction, as well as other life forms that once thrived there. This has everything to do with the information that you need at this time.

We have spoken of the Dolphin Beings—of their weaving of the frequencies of the oceans. As they disappear from your planet, the oceans are becoming more unruly, more devastating. The Great Whales are peacefully committing mass suicide alongside of them, for they too are no longer capable of holding resonance with the emotional body of Gaia.

They are preparing the way for their extinction, knowing that they can no longer serve you. Most of humankind has simply never understood what they came to give you.

Be aware that the water, great conductor of electromagnetic frequencies, has been altered at that level as well—its wam vibration is so affected by the electromagnetic interference that now permeates all earth space. Even the underground wells, once sacred and pure, are becoming tainted with the toxins of human waste. You can no longer depend upon the "well" for purity and life-enhancing energies.

What can be done, you ask us?

Know that individually, your efforts are too scattered and the human voice is too weak. Stopgap measures, treatment plants, and purification methods are far too limited and too focused on the material realm to be of any real significance.

To heal the waters of Gaia, you must now unite forces and work on etheric planes, where the focused intent of all lightwork teams unites under one objective: the reestablishment of harmonic overtones of the music of the seas in dynamic synthesis with the elements of fire, air, and earth. That is the key.

Earth's wam vibration, the music of Gaia's soul, must be cleared of the electromagnetic pulse of destruction, rage, and the violent mind.

You can call upon the ascended Dolphin Beings and Great Whales for guidance, if you are open to receiving them at the telepathic, empathic levels. They will come. They can reach you on many levels.

Therefore, bring the word, the music, the light, and your knowledge through the writing and the selected works of others, just as you bring forth your own visions—for this is your mission. Be sure to allow your emotional experience of this most important issue to flow through you, allowing the expression to take form as it moves through you, trusting that you are guided and assisted on all levels.

Many experts tell us that the changes that are occurring now have actually occurred before and, clearly, the Earth survived. Please guide us in understanding how our contemporary crises are different than global changes in the past and, hence, how our outcome will be this time around.

We are in agreement as to the cyclical nature of geophysical forces on your planet. You are a technologically advancing society capable of recording, reading, and analyzing earth records, as they pertain to geophysical, atmospheric, and climatic changes and you are now able to document similar eras in the tumultuous evolution of Planet Earth.

What your geophysicists are missing in their evaluation of your global alterations is how they reflect the emotional nature of Gaia's expression ... for they do not see her as a living, conscious being and so they do not connect the consciousness to the events. There lies the essence of your dilemma.

Nor do they understand the interrelationships of celestial beings ... of Ra, your Sun, and his true relationship with Earth ... of the multidimensional awareness that both hold of themselves, celestial beings, and their existence in the multiverse.

In answer to your question: yes, much of what is occurring now has happened before the geological period you know as the "Holocene."

This frame of reference refers to the last ten thousand radiocarbon years or so, although we wish to be more precise by describing it as the era following the demise of Atlantis.

During this expanse of "time," your planetary body has endured extreme alterations and, of these, water has been the most dramatically altered element. Water is the emotion—the emotional body—of Gaia.

At the onset of the Holocene period, Gaia manifested her rage and emotional upheaval with the collapse of the ice sheets, which left enormous quantities of subglacial waters flowing into the oceans. Huge masses of icebergs migrated into the warmer ocean waters. The flow streams within the oceans were altered along with the multitude of life forms that held the vibrations there: the Great Whales, the Dolphin Beings, and all other sea creatures.

This enormous shift produced catastrophic rises in sea levels, which in turn dramatically affected the climatic patterns of the planet. All atmospheric rhythms were reversed and your world, in more than just a metaphorical sense, was turned upside down.

This is occurring again now.

Earth's ice sheets are de-stabilizing and soon will collapse entirely; the Arctic and Antarctic regions are breaking apart, sending huge glacial masses afloat in the oceans, and the flow lines of the sea energy streams are changing.

Great chasms are opening in the ocean floors while volcanic explosions are occurring continuously at every nerve center of the planet.

Rivers are changing their course—this is all too clear in the Amazonian regions of your planet.

The great difference between this era and that immediately following the fall of Atlantis is that your planet is preparing to leave the physical plane in which it still holds resonance, however discordant. That is the ultimate contrast between these, the Desert Days of Planet Earth, and those catastrophic epochs that have come before you.

You are preparing for lift-off. And this, too, you will survive.

It seems all of our problems are immortalized in the misconduct of the Atlanteans. Just what was so terribly wrong with that civilization to have created such devastation?

Over the many millennia that define the third cycle, the world of the Atlanteans shifted uncontrollably away from the spiritual pursuits that had identified the first generations.

The Annunaki intervened heavy-handedly in the late days of Atlantis and their influence, enforced through their electromagnetic stimulation of the lower chakras and mind-control technologies, stimulated ego consciousness and separated the spiritual leadership—pushing the populace to worship the material and driving society into ideological separation. They altered the values and perceptions of the Atlantean people by building upon their primordial fear of survival, creating conflict and wars, and by introducing sacrificial rites into the culture.

These, the darkest acts of forced submission, involved violent and public death for those whose misfortune it was to be "chosen" by the Dark Priesthood, who operated under the hypnotic influence of their Annunaki lords. With the flow of human blood into communal temple grounds, the life force of the Atlanteans— their collective will—was drawn from their beings, while the sacred spaces suffocated under the weight of human despair and violence.

The lightworkers of the later generations found they simply could not neutralize the intention of the insipid dark warriors, who were so exceptionally focused and manipulating that the entire culture slipped, almost unknowingly, into the dark chasm of their secret rule.

With time, the pendulum swung so completely into the shadows that the only possibility for Earth—and the human race— was to bring it all down and start anew. That was the time of the Last Generation, the apex point of the third cycle of Atlantis, when all was brought to winter: to rest and to be cleansed there, in the deep waters of your collective experience.

When you understand the cyclical nature of all life in the material realms, you realize that such events are a natural process and that this has been the way of Earth's immortality. There is a certain comfort in knowing that all energies eventually move towards center, where the fury of opposition transforms into the serenity of balance point. All things reach their peak, crash, and come up again, at the meridian.

Such is the design of life; such is its cyclical nature.

Have we learned from this colossal error, I ask myself, or are we even more distant from understanding what we create? Your teachings leave me wondering if we have learned our lessons. It certainly does not seem so, given the state of our world.

Do not underestimate the evolutionary strides that your race has taken, despite the chaos that appears to reign in your realm.

The Atlanteans' ability to attune to the vibrational frequencies of the celestial deities and their innate understanding of the Gaian energies have been passed down from generation to generation—around the globe, for the impact of that civilization altered the nature of all human consciousness.

Their knowledge, held by the Keepers of the Records as the "Secret Wisdom," has been carried by the Wise Ones of great civilizations and tribal communities, there where the truth of indigenous peoples has neither been ravaged by the omnipotent nor sacrificed to materialism and the disintegration of human values.

You, the New Aquarians, appreciate the nature of the celestial beings; this is a reawakening of your innate understanding of galactic consciousness. You are bringing balance, hope, and visions of a new paradigm while reviving the lessons of the past.

Celebrate your accomplishments, for they are vast and far-reaching, and know that the desperate events occurring in your global societies are actually pushing the greater body of beings to release from their unconscious obedience and take responsibility for the New World.

Are you alluding to the fact that we are due for a pole shift, as prophesized by the great mystics of the past?

At this writing, a little more than one calendar year from the moment of the immense tectonic shift in your southeastern seas, the wobble in Earth's spin axis has basically stopped—there is currently little or no wobble in Earth's rotation.

The axis of your planet has already begun to shift and will continue to slide as all is revolutionized in your world.

This shift has been attributed to the enormous quake in that part of your world, but in truth it is far more complex than that.

Your Sun's shifting magnetic fields are wielding dramatic energy shifts within the body of Gaia, causing the electromagnetic flow lines within the Earth to change their orientation.

This, too, is part of the process of your planet's ascension and although it may be frightening to you—it is a natural part of your journey: something like the unborn infant when it shifts position in preparation for delivery through the birth tunnel.

So you do agree that the Earth is beginning to reverse its poles, but we don't really know what that will mean to us. Can you elaborate to us what is happening, in actuality, to cause such upheaval on our planet?

We understand that human destruction and abuse of our resources have a primary role in our accelerating disharmony, but I am eager to know what you, the viewers, see occurring from your galactic perspective.

The situation is filled with complexity and varying levels of duality that are intensely representative of the enormous evolutionary leaps that your planet and those of your solar family are undertaking at this point.

Yes, human behavior has dramatically accelerated the decline of countless species of life on your planet, as it has reduced the quality of life at most locations on the surface. And yet, at the other end of the spectrum, it has given life to countless new species, which thrive on the new electromagnetic, chemical, and biological environments that have been created from such imbalances.

This is the way of life throughout the Cosmos: life dies, life is born anew.

From the galactic perspective, we understand that as your Sun, Ra, prepares to ascend from his physical manifestation in the dense three-dimensional reality, his accelerating electromagnetic fields are going to eventually flip altogether: this is marked by the next surge in solar flare activity which occurs, not surprisingly, in 2012.

The Sun's reversal, the huge proton storms that will occur, and the immensity of those solar showers mark the end of that vibration of male-dominant, fear-based consciousness that still holds you in separation, as well as the renewal of the nurturing yin frequencies that will guide you through the changes.

This process will dramatically alter the electromagnetic flow lines of all the Earth, from the mineral kingdom to the plants, animals, and humans, whose electromagnetic energy grids will also experience extraordinary power surges. This is why it is of such importance that you do the work of clearing the miasmas that still block your energy networks, as you will need to be able to let these energies flow through you. You will need to be clear channels.

The changing solar magnetism will cause huge surges in the hormonal secretions that activate the pineal gland. This is a clue to your personal ascension processes.

Yes, there will be great change, we do not deny that. There will be desertification of great expanses of land just as there will be flooding; there will be destruction as there will be renewal; there will be panic as there will be acceptance. All depends upon your understanding of change as evolution and your awareness that all moves upward on the spiral of light.

Can you tell us, in simple terms, what will be the most significant and pressing manifestation of climate change on our planet and how best we can deal with it?

No one aspect of the shift will be significant to all the living of Earth, for your planet is a rich tapestry of varied ecosystems. However, we can tell you that the most devastation will manifest in two polar experiences. On the one hand, flood waters will soon overtake your coastal areas, redefining the topography of the continents—just as they will deluge the densely populated areas at sea level and within twenty kilometers of the rivers. On the other, encroaching desertification will drive huge human, animal, and plant populations to famine.

These are expressions of the extreme duality in which you find yourselves, and their effects are already beginning to be felt across the planet.

How can you deal with it?

Contribute to the healing of Gaia with your hearts, your minds, your hands, your souls and stay grounded in the knowledge that believing your world can be better will make it so.

Be aware, but not afraid.

Be in love, not anger.

And trust that, despite appearances, Gaia knows what to do. Do you?

What are gravitational waves and how are they affecting the Earth Changes?

Gravitational waves are current streams in the weave of consciousness upon which the space-time construct is formed. They breeze through the Cosmos, like galactic winds, forming distortions in the construct and altering the dynamics of celestial harmonics, like ripples in the lake. They are neither responsible for the changes occurring on Earth, nor are they affecting Ra's revolution.

6

Agharta: The Inner World

Of wondrous possibilities, we wish to speak to you now of a Utopian land of beauty and light—one that, unbeknownst to most of the human race, actually exists in Earth's contemporary physical reality.

In the deep inner world of Gaia, there lives a bustling, thriving civilization of highly evolved beings—descendants of the first Atlantean colonizers of the underground. Protected from the geophysical disturbance and upheaval that has swept your surface world for so many millions of years, the Atlanteans not only survived the last great Ice Age, but went on to create a superb world in the womb of the Earth Mother ... a land of the yin vibration.

A land known as **Agharta**.

The idea of a great underground civilization is no whimsical hypothesis. The world of Agharta and its cultural center, Shambhala, are well known to studied Buddhists and Tibetan Lamas, and many are the mystics and visionaries who have "seen" these lands and traveled there in light body.

The fortunate and the chosen of your spirit leaders regularly visit there in physical form. Theirs is an extensive knowledge of the highly evolved world of the inner Earth, for they are frequent visitors to Shambhala, where they receive guidance and direction to bring back to the surface from the priests of the White Brotherhood presiding in this realm. Sages of many epochs have brought through the wisdom and brilliance of the idyllic civilization that flourishes below, and the knowledge sits in your collective consciousness, awaiting recognition.

Throughout earth time, diverse civilizations have interacted with these Atlantean super beings, for there are still tunnel openings at various points on the planet and there have been visitations from the Aghartans at various crucial points in "surface time." At pivotal moments in Earth's history, select societies, such as the Lemurians, Tibetans, the Maya, ancient Egyptians, the Druids, and Etruscans, were visited by Aghartan spirit leaders, who brought their wisdom to the surface to assist the souls transiting the outer world and to serve Gaia's higher purpose.

Of these, the Tibetans, many of whom are the reincarnated souls of the Atlanteans of the second cycle or direct descendants of the third cycle Atlanteans, had open contact until the middle of your last century, when the Bodhisattva, Dalai Lama, was forced to flee those sacred lands forever. The Tibetan portal in the spiritual vortex of Lhasa was sealed with his departure, to be replaced with one that extends from India through to the base of Mt. Kailash, and it is from here that journeys to Shambhala are still embarked upon by select Tibetan leaders—those who have been chosen to serve as messengers.

Atlantis Rising

You have discussed the advanced civilization of Agharta—the inner Earth—in your second book. In it, you explain that the first cycle Atlanteans migrated into the Earth after a global Ice Age and estab-

lished the first Aghartan colonies. Wouldn't they have returned to surface once the planet thawed? This remains a mystery to me.

With the retreat of the ice layers, teams of Aghartan explorers did indeed return to the surface—strangers to a world their ancestors had been forced to leave behind. This was a natural extension of human curiosity: a need to seek out that which has yet to be "found" as much as that which has been, in a sense, "lost," and the subconscious desire to reach out to your galactic family and return to the stars.

Many Sirian souls chose to generate form upon the Earth at that time to assist in the rebirthing of the human race and to help reactivate your direct connection with the Family of Light. The Yzhnüni, whom we speak of in that material, were the first to materialize in the early days of human return.

Despite the Aghartans' recorded knowledge of Earth's circadian rhythms, their ability to understand the stars and celestial beings, their experience of night and day, the lunar cycle, the seasons, and the Sun required an overwhelming adjustment in consciousness and sensorial perception. They did, with time, adapt and mutate in the physical body to the bright light and harsh conditions of the Atlantean highlands—their point of emergence.

This they accomplished in various stages: first, by retreating back into cave shelters in the strongest phases of solar radiation, violent weather, and geophysical stress-activated phenomena. Later, they constructed granite fortresses to serve as temples and communal dwellings, where they spent most of the daylight hours … until they were strong enough to withstand the natural forces of the new environment.

The first wave of Aghartan explorers appeared at approximately 27,500 BC. With time there were others, lured by tales of the New World, and more followed, in waves of migration that spanned a period of over five hundred years. They were pioneers—founders of the New Atlantis, which sprang back to life approximately one thousand years after their ancestors had deserted the continent in search of salvation in the womb of Mother Earth.

The third cycle of Atlantis had begun.

Theirs was a golden age, a time of celebration and rebirth. Undaunted by the hardships they encountered in the surface world, the New Atlanteans were bold adventurers, physically superior beings, from whom the archetypal heroes of later generations were modeled. The challenges of rebuilding a civilization were vast, yet they were eager and they were determined, for they knew it was their karmic return.

Moreover, their emergence from the womb brought the stimulation of the yang vibration to exaltation, activating men and women alike in their forward thrust—the most determined of adventures in the surface world they had come to reclaim.

Of such infinite strength and beauty were the boundless rivers, majestic mountain peaks, the Sun, and stars that the people soon created iconic gods of all the forces of nature. They established elaborate rites of worship and, eventually, hierarchies of gods came to dominate their spiritual lives—whereas the Aghartans, their ancestors, practiced the pursuit of inner balance and the resolution of polarity as individuals and the greater whole.

Nonetheless ... emerging from a world in which there were no seasons, no climatic variations, no stars nor moon, the newcomers to the surface were understandably awed by the magnificence and they bowed before the expressions of Gaian beauty and the greater cosmic forces.

The new civilization advanced rapidly, for this was a time of expansion and reconstruction. Life in the new habitat, lain dormant from the thousand-year freeze, once again burst into Gaian spring and, like their ancestors, the New Atlanteans discovered endless varieties of flora and fauna never before experienced in their respective lands. Of these, there were predatory species roaming the land in search of food, and others, which lived in the waters. In the below, where no being destroys another, this was a curious aspect of the new reality that faced them.

Still, the first Atlanteans to appear from the caves were determined to survive their new-found adversities and to remain. Their spirit and expansive heart centers were the foundations of the new society, and these loving energies would mark Atlantean culture for many millennia to follow.

They worshipped the celestial bodies, reflecting the light of the heavens, the elemental beings, the song that whispered in the wind. The beauty of the outer world was immense—well worth the challenges of an environment they had yet to understand.

There were floods, violent storms, and raging winds, phenomena they had never known, but only remotely remembered in myth, woven from the tales of the ancestors. There were the animals, to whom they were prey. Indeed, contrary to the serenity and harmony of Agharta, the world they had come to rediscover and rebuild was as harsh and unyielding as it was filled with the laughter and light of the gods.

The average life expectancy, which had once embraced many

centuries of linear time, plummeted by hundreds of years and the generations that followed the first pioneers were faced with drastic new perceptions of death and dying.

In the strange new world, the early pioneers soon began to believe in their vulnerability and to beg mercy of their gods. These were emotions and behaviors they had never known in the safety of the world below. In times of great upheaval in the forces of nature, they eventually learned to feel victimized and unworthy—and to create their own impotence.

So it was that fear first manifested in the people of the New World. Many chose to retreat back to the warmth and beauty of the inner world, where the light is perennial and Spirit prevails.

I would like to know what is happening there now and how the Aghartans are involved with us on the surface. Will they be interacting and merging with us before we pass through?

The world of Agharta is a highly developed society of technically advanced, spiritually evolved beings who live in peace and celebration within the golden light of the inner Earth.

Like you, they are dedicated to raising their young, nurturing the living beings that share their world, traveling the path of spiritual enlightenment, and making their lives meaningful and fulfilling.

Aghartans are preparing to receive envoys of the enlightened amongst you before your passage into the fourth. This is already under way, as some of you are well aware.

There are telepathic communications, as there are special frequency "radio" waves coming to the surface, which some channels are able to bring through for you ... as our instrument does for us at determined intervals of our earthly communications.

There are the true spirit leaders of your planet, who come and go from the land of Shambhala, bringing you the Wisdom and the inner earth codes. They are the guardians of the musical patterns of the inner Earth—the wam vibration of the Gaian soul.

It is very difficult to believe that a civilization could exist underground, without the benefit of the Sun's light. It certainly is unimaginable that a race of underworld beings could be confined to the darkness of the inner world and at the same time be considered the "enlightened race" of man. Maybe I'm just a skeptic.

Perhaps your skepticism has prevented you from examining possibilities where you have convinced yourself they do not or cannot exist—and that shuts down the probing of the curious mind.

What you believe is unimaginable, you may soon discover, is based on a wrong assumption—your certainty that darkness fills the womb of the Earth—where, conversely, light abounds!

Let us examine what you really do know about the center of your world.

With all of the technological advances of your contemporary civilization, human beings are capable of surviving in space in permanent stations there; you have created underground cities and transportation systems in your major urban areas; you have built bunkers and survival systems that can hold against total nuclear annihilation, providing for the long-term underground residence of your political and wealthy elite; you can live underwater, walk on the moon, and probe the far reaches of your solar system.

Yet, you find it "unimaginable" that a civilization of Atlanteans, the most technologically advanced race ever to walk your Earth, could find its way into the Earth's center and use their knowledge and experience there to create a new Atlantis—a world reborn?

We tell you that it is so—just as the earth sages have hinted to you from time immemorial.

In the deep of the inner Earth, the thriving spiritual center of Gaia abounds with light, untainted food sources, crystalline, conscious water, and the natural beauty of pristine forests, lakes, oceans, and self-sustaining urban communities.

Everywhere, love for Gaia abounds.

All living beings—the humans (for human they are), the animals, the trees, and plants—live in harmony and all understand and are committed to the peaceful co-existence of all species. The rich mineral kingdom provides untold energy sources for the cities and communities of the enlightened Atlanteans. All have learned to transcend their sense of separateness, beyond the limitations of the ego and the illusive boundaries of space and time.

You might recognize how your surface societies have for so long been focused on the superficial aspects of life. They, the inner earth dwellers, have gone deeply within themselves, searching to find the oneness of the cosmic soul.

As to the previous question of their interaction with the beings of the surface, know that the hidden spiritual leaders amongst you do enter the sacred walls of Shambhala (both physically and astrally) and they do receive guidance for the human race dwelling upon the surface.

The road to Agharta is universal to the true spirit seeker: detachment from possession; respect for all life; silencing of the chattering mind ... the opening of the One Heart. But only those who are called are able to enter those hallowed gates ... only the true Masters.

What about the Hollow Earth theory? How does this fit with the idea that such a civilization exists near the center of the Earth?

Your Earth is not hollow from north to south poles, as has been suggested in some of your recent texts. This is merely a holographic projection that serves as a shield to those interested in entering, uninvited, into the sacred lands of Agharta.

If, however, you intend that to mean that it is not a solid sphere—a density of ore and rock—then yes ... yes, indeed. Once you get through the outer passageways, you quickly discover that the inner world of Gaia is a golden bowl of light, pulsating in exquisite rhythm with every celestial body in the heavens and resonating to the music of love.

Is it true that there are extraterrestrials underground—are they citizens of Agharta?

Alien species are found in the primary subsurface levels, where your surface government elite have burrowed in to build their private earthways: fortresses, weapons silos, intercontinental speed railways, laboratories, storage centers, and military bases.

You must not confuse the "underground" with the inner world of Gaia.

As we have previously stated, aliens do work there, in the sub-terranean levels, just as they have created living environments in the depths of your oceans, where they remain relatively hidden to all but the myriad sea beings who share the waterways of the Great Whales and the Dolphin Beings.

You are only now beginning to learn that there are indeed craft of extraterrestrial origin entering and exiting their subterranean and suboceanic bases.

But there, in the deep inner world of Agharta, there are no alien races, for they cannot penetrate. Only the highly evolved intra-terrestrial *Homo sapiens* populate the protected world: Atlantean settlers from the closing of the second cycle of Atlantean civilization, with the Ice Age—approximately thirty-five thousand earth years ago.

It is believed that there do actually exist elaborate tunnels into Agharta from various points of entry in South and North America, Europe, and specifically Tibet. Can you verify this?

Tunnels that lead to Agharta are found in every land mass of your planet, with a key entry port located at the pole—as experienced by your Admiral Byrd, who actually reached the inner world and lived to return and speak of the wonders he beheld there.

From the most remote Himalayan peaks, to the most heavily populated urban centers, portals exist from which Aghartans do exit from time to time ... but rarely are humans allowed entry.

These points of passage are protected by an energy source known to the Atlanteans—the mindlight generators—which were capable of harvesting the conscious thoughts and focused will of the collective for the creation and storage of what we will refer to as "environmental magnetism."

This energy alters the vibration of matter at the inner portals to the point that anyone intent upon entering without invitation would, were (s)he astute enough to locate and enter a tunnel, experience confusion, disorientation, and even death.

This force has been identified by your mystics as the "Vril Power." It is the use of the collective consciousness of the few or the many to alter the material realm, just as it was used in Atlantis to create all the needed energy to power entire cities.

Tunnels in and out of Agharta can be closed and opened at the will of the leadership, as determined by the energetic vibrations of the surface locations and any threat to the inner world.

Such is the case now with the portal in Tibet, where the exquisite energy of the spirit leaders has been all but erased by the aggressors, who have disrupted the power of peace and destroyed the harmonies that once resonated across the mountaintops of the Himalayan Range.

Are you suggesting that Aghartans walk amongst us?

We are declaring that at certain points of your globe, particularly those places you know as India, Tibet, Mongolia, the Andes, and the high northern hemispheres, Aghartan scouts have exited and entered the gateways to gather information regarding the outer world, yes, and that at key times in your evolution they have interacted with beings from select societies, such as: the Egyptians, the Tibetans, the Druids, the Maya, and native peoples of many continents.

They remain imprinted on the myths and legends of these peoples and you can find reference everywhere around you, in the carvings upon stone and the oral traditions that remain with the Keepers of the Records.

However, we are not suggesting that they walk the streets of your twenty-first-century cities, disguised as your contemporaries. Aside from their distinct physical forms, which would unquestionably set them apart from you all, they would not be able to withstand the environmental pollution, the bacteria, and viruses with which you share your common spaces and the very air you breathe.

Highly telepathic, they cannot withstand the negative vibration of the current mass consciousness of outer earth residents.

May we know what these people look like?

They are of the extremely fair complexion of your Nordic races, of great height, with lean bodies (they stand twice the average height of contemporary human beings) and a keen instinct. Their sensory apparati are far more acute than yours and their eyes are huge by your standards, reflecting the high-end spectrum hues of blue-violet and magenta.

They enjoy extremely long life spans—centuries long—and live in robust good health and well-being, reflected in their youthful appearance and glowing energy fields.

Is there both a physical and nonphysical Agharta? With so many people experiencing this place on astral planes, it is a question I often ask myself.

The call goes out in the ethers—those of you who are invited hear the bells ringing and you enter the astral planes of Agharti to receive the teachings you are meant to bring back to your communities. For some, this is a conscious process; for others, it is veiled to the conscious mind and yet you retrieve the experience from your subconscious and bring it forward in your spirit work.

Know that all that is manifest in the physical world is projected in the astral—including, of course, your very being: your "I am" awareness.

If you find yourself in the land of Shambhala in dreams, astral journeys, and other meditative and altered states, you may well one day find you have actually entered there in body.

Many of you are preparing for this, consciously and not, by undertaking your journeys to the sacred sites of Gaia. You are receiving the codes, unraveling the secrets ... that lead to Agharta.

Isn't there a danger that with all the underground drilling and development the power elite may just find their way into the sacred lands?

No. There is no port of entry, deliberate or accidental, for the unwelcome. All attempts by the Secret Government to enter have been thwarted and we assure you that there is no world more protected from invasion or forced entry.

Only the spirit masters of the surface world can find their way through the labyrinth and into the inner sanctum. They alone are pure enough to bring the outer world into their sacred passageways, to be cleansed in the Vril waves and healed at the gateways of Agharta.

What will be the Aghartan role in the imminent ascension of Gaia? Will the surface and inner worlds merge?

Cosmic rays traverse the outer crust of the body of Earth, just as they do your bodies, and so there is a natural transmutation of life energies there as well. However, whereas the large majority of outer earth dwellers work against Gaia, the Aghartans' love and understanding of earth energies work **with** her ... hence, their experience of galactic current streams and shifting earth manifestations is as gentle as the wind on the willows.

They are the fetus in the womb of the nurturing mother—hearing the noise of the outer world, feeling the bumps and pains, but knowing only unconditional love, safety, and anticipation.

For those of Agharta—you understand—ascension is understood to be the conclusion of millennia of "gestation" and the long-awaited time of birth.

The celebrations have begun. The towns, the villages, the cities, and everywhere in between are filled with anticipation, as all prepare for the great reunion with the galactic Family of Light.

7

The Gifts of Ancients

From my understanding, ancient Egypt seems almost to be a planet by itself. It seems to have developed at an extraordinary rate compared to others of the same time period—not surprising, since its population were survivors of Atlantis. They seem to be the most extensive organized society of that period and well in advance in many aspects to other civilizations of that time.

Since the end of Atlantis was known well in advance, was it decided on your part (the Sirian and other High Councils) to simply concentrate or continue the knowledge of Atlantis in one place on Earth, because of what was going to happen in the future?

We remind you that every soul of every realm of consciousness exists as master of its own destiny at the individual level, and as a vibrationally attuned co-creator of the collective experience. As earth residents of the third dimension, you are co-creators of the earth experience. Earth, in turn, co-creates the experience of your stellar being, Ra, of which it is, yet again, an aspect and a reflection.

We, intelligence of higher dimensions, focus upon the events playing out in our realities, which are inevitably the result of those souls who have evolved to this point on the spiral of consciousness along with us. However, as all is One in the Cosmos of Soul, the consciousness of every level, every individual, and every dimension is a reflection of the whole. Therefore, we are both affected by your reality and effective in it as well.

It is neither our desire nor our responsibility to decide what is to happen in the playing out of events in your realm, for that would be an act of altering your karmic process, as well as our own.

Rather, we have served at various intervals in certain evolutionary fields in order that we might shine more light down into the spiral, where those who climb from the various degrees of darkness and shadow lands are enabled to see more clearly what lies ahead—where the light becomes brighter with every step.

As to the question of Atlantis, we ask that you consider that the knowledge of that ancient world was not limited to the lands of ancient Egypt—the Khemit. Rather, it was spread to many locations upon the Earth, for the continent of Atlantis reached from its northern shores, icy and cold, to its southernmost tip, far below the steamy equatorial regions, and so enjoyed access and contact with indigenous populations of every imaginable description and place.

We believe that you are realizing this now, as you are discovering Atlantean philosophies, constructs, magic, and astronomical alignments in almost every continent of your modern world. You are recognizing the recurring themes in the ancient stories. Much is coming to light now about your true origins, your true DNA coding, and soon the secrets of Atlantis—and all that occurred there—will be revealed as well.

The Hall of Records beneath the Great Sphinx has already been located—but it has yet to be activated. Another secret chamber lies within the pyramid itself—this too has been discovered but has yet to reveal its purpose, for those who currently hold the keys to the gates are not of the light and they come to the experience without love. They dig madly in the solar fields of the Giza energy complex, unable to put the pieces together, for fragments of their own souls are scattered, like shards upon the sands of time.

Do not fear or create dark illusions in your minds. Master lightworkers of your great planet will be enabled to activate Giza and all the other Atlantean power stations when it is time to open the Halls. As the shifting sands of history have hidden, so have they revealed, awaiting the right coordinates on the time-space continuum. All is in perfect order as you approach the point of your acceleration out of the density and into the light.

The thirteen Atlantean crystal skulls will be reunited at that time. The mindlight generators of Atlantis will illuminate the underworld. The Halls of Amenti will begin to materialize before your eyes. This, all of this, will occur in your lifetimes.

We ask you always to bear in mind that much of this monumental wisdom, knowledge, and technology of the Atlantean experience was light-filled, while some was very dark in its intent—for throughout the millennia of Atlantis there were continuous cycles of darkness and light—in their ultimate intensity—and one of those cycles of extremes is now playing out in your contemporary earth experience: the Desert Days.

Of this emergent Atlantean record, none remains more indelibly coded and secreted than in Egypt, where the records of your planet's experience are safely stored and encoded and so much has survived the ravages and destruction of time, the shifting of the Earth's form, and the human hand. There lie so many buried secrets, disguised in the myths of the gods, which evolve from the early times of the third cycle of Atlantis—when Osiris (of Sirius) and his Atlantean Queen Isis reigned in the resurrected lands of that great land.

This we will soon reveal to you, knowing there will be controversy and resistance ... aware of what we will evoke in those who cling to the belief systems of contemporary thought and declared expert historians.

At the time of the final catastrophe of Atlantis, over ten thousand earth years before the Christed One walked the earth and twenty thousand years after their ancestors had burned the path, significant other numbers of the White Brotherhood escaped the catastrophe at the surface through the intricate tunnel networks and cities of inner Earth.

Some resurfaced in the lands of Khemit, where it was divined that there would be created all the record halls needed for the survival of the Atlantean record and perhaps, the very human race itself. Others fled to the Mayalands, the high grounds of Tibet and Peru ... all with a mission to preserve the light of the Ancient Sun.

Dark Ones followed, for we remind you yet again that there is always darkness and light in the density of the third dimension. It is the nature of your reality. What you do with these vibrations, both as individuals and as a collective, is what determines the "future" as you know it and that is not the work nor the responsibility of those beyond your realm—although we do what we can to assist in your passage out of the darkness and into the light. We too have passed there. We too were aided by those further along, and so it goes.

Bearing in mind that your purpose along the journey is just as much to extend a hand to those who trail behind as it is to reach to the one just ahead, you learn the true significance of light-working for the greatest good of all.

We ask you always to remember, as well, that the future (as you know it) is never pre-determined and that all is forever changing in the illusory world in which you dwell.

The past is an illusion—for it is a swirling canvas of memory in movement—and it is different for every single one of you.

The future is an illusion—for it is mere conjecture and it is of the one and the many, malleable, changing with every karmic act.

And the present, illusive, flees from your mind just as quickly as it comes into being.

Was Egypt a land of immortality and planned that way?

Pre-dynastic Egypt was a time of pure Atlantean and Sirian influence upon the receptive indigenous tribes of the Khemit, where the history of Atlantean existence and evolution was brought to manifestation. Through the use of sound, conscious thought, and light, the spiritual indigenous people were shown the wonders of far more ancient days, while the wonders of their own were integrated into a new form—the Egyptian High Culture. These works, pre- and post-Atlantean Khemitian records, are very much a part of the great works of your Egyptian ancestors, and they are intertwined throughout the myths.

What was "planned" for humanity was of a two-fold purpose: one, to immortalize the record of all that came "before" (symbolized by the left eye of Horus) and the other to serve to awaken and activate that consciousness for what lay ahead of you (symbolized by the right).

Despite attempts by historians to conceal the truth of the Atlantean legacy, you no doubt have gleaned from all that has been left for you that the immensity of Egypt's high culture, with its profound knowledge and technology, does not fit the "time line" of the archeological record.

We speak of that construct on the space-time continuum that marked the "end" of the third cycle of Atlantis and the "beginning" of the high society of Egypt, which declined, in focus and spirit, with each new dynasty, as the land of ancient Egypt. However, we ask you to bear in mind that traces of the Great Civilization of Atlantis—when Osiris walked—still exist in Egypt and that it is the memory and discovery of the Osiris cult that mark the intervention of the Great Atlanteans in Khemit.

That generation of Atlanteans, you are soon to discover, was far more important than the last and it is their contribution that is most important to you now.

It is best to clarify that by "land of immortality" we understand your question to mean that you wish to know if it was intended that Egypt serve as the storehouse of the Atlantean wisdom from which it sprang forth and flourished. We confirm to you that it has indeed been constructed so that the secrets of humanity's passing through the greatest hours of its existence on the earth plane would remain safeguarded, until such time as the human race would reach the level of understanding to decipher the coded wisdom, activate the keys of multidimensional experience, and utilize it all for the highest good of Gaia and worlds beyond.

Through its unlimited archeological record and rich mythological legends, Egypt reveals to the Initiate the spiritual mastery and wisdom of the highest societies of ancient Atlantis, just as it holds the keys to the story of the last generations. It is all there, immortalized in stone and in the unspoken word, for you to peer into as a living tapestry of what you believe is past—and to unravel and activate—as a gateway to the new dawn. A more perfect reflection of its immortality cannot be found!

This is our understanding of your question regarding the intention that Egypt be an immortal land, for in continuing the legacy of Atlantis and projecting it into your contemporary consciousness, it has indeed rendered Atlantis and its people immortal in your experience.

If, instead, your question is intended to mean a "land of immortality" where the focus of life was preparation for the eternal life of the soul, with the resurrection of the physical being—let us say to you "yes, the quest for immortality of the soul and the resurrection of the physical being were the quintessential focus of life in ancient Egypt."

From the myths of the "first time" or Zep Tepi, as described in Egyptian texts, early religious cults of Egypt taught that, like Osiris, the individual could achieve immortality and retain a physical essence in the afterlife. This quest for life eternal, misinterpreted from the earliest stories of Osiris and his otherworldly presence so many millennia prior, was unquestionably an overriding theme in the evolution of Egyptian culture.

What remains today, in the evidence brought forward from the tombs of old, are symbols of the Egyptians' search to achieve immortality, obtained through three distinct processes. The first was the mummification of the body, painstakingly undertaken to preserve the physical form. The second was to provide all the essentials that would be required by the spirit on its passing: nourishment, tools, and personal items of significance to the departing one. The third required incantations and magical spells that remained buried with the body so that the spirit could rise from the body and journey to the Halls of Amenti.

The pursuit of eternal life is a recurring theme throughout the human experience, for it is you remembering, at the primordial level, that the disempowering idea of finality—your death—is only an illusion and that the soul is eternal.

What was the specific role of the Sirians at the time of Osiris, Isis, and Horus?

The question of our presence at this point of the story of Atlantis/Egypt is complex and one that requires significant elaboration—which we are preparing to do with our channel in the upcoming work, *Where Pharaohs Dwell,* evolving from her time at the Holy of Holies.

There are many layers, many aspects to the story and so many clues have been left for you—almost all of which have been misinterpreted by historians.

Often in your search for answers regarding your multidimensional existence, you overlook the fact that the illuminated masters amongst you have shown you the art of materializing, de-materializing, and rearranging the Atum to create new forms. You ask yourselves, "Did gods truly descend from the heavens to walk amongst us?" and ponder their intervention, as well as ours, in your worlds. In the case of the Osiris legend, it is one and the same.

Osiris (anagram of Sirios) was a master of light from the Sirian star system who made his entry into your world through a portal created early on, at the beginning of the third cycle of Atlantis. We have elaborated this information in our prior work, *Atlantis Rising,* describing how beings of Yzhnüni, a Sirian satellite, retrograded into your dimension to serve in the evolution of the Atlanteans.

> *We reiterate that the third and final cycle began with the melting of the ice sheets. As the glaciers began their rapid retreat from the continent, a great flourishing occurred rather spontaneously and Atlantis, one of the last land masses to experience the devastation, was one of the first to be revitalized ... both energetically and climatically. Many Sirian souls chose to generate upon the Earth at that time to assist in the rebirthing of the human race as part of our karmic bond with you, and to settle our unresolved karmic issues with the Annunaki of Nebiru. We were able to read the Akashic Record and observed that the Family of Light would be called into Earth's fields at that time, and so it was believed, in a sense, to be our destiny to incarnate below our vibration in a return to the third dimension.*
>
> *This was a time when the first Sirians appeared as humanoids upon the face of the Earth, specifically in the mountain lands of Atlantis. Like our Solar Deity, Satais (Sirius B), the planet body of their origin, Yzhnü, is no longer of*

*the material universe, for it resonates at a higher frequency—
a six-dimensional planetary essence which exists in a parallel
universe alongside of yours. For the Yzhnüni, it was a chance
to live again in form, with all the challenges consciously evolving beings would face from the elements, the other life forms,
and the transmutational process of retrogradation, while resolv-
ing the karma that, binding Sirius to the Gaian vibration,
would have forever delayed our own evolution.*

*The Yzhnüni, starseed of Sirius, experienced great diffi-
culty crystallizing in the third dimension, for theirs was a
vibration which had long before passed from physicality, and
the return to material form was riddled with uncertainty.
Yet, reports of the blue-green planet, her majesty and music,
sang through the universe and her fascination was immense.
Quite simply, Gaia was the siren of the heavens and these
Sirian souls were the Ulysses of the galactic seas.*

*Their essence crystallized in the three-dimensional fields
of earth reality as very tall, radiant hominids, of a form that
closely resembled human anatomy and structure ... but
which clearly was not. Most distinguishing were their extensive auric fields, which emanated visibly many feet beyond
their physical bodies. Their outer coverings were like a delicate foil, absolutely white and translucent, so that to the
natives they appeared as fairy-like beings and were perceived
as such for many centuries of their existence in the earth
sphere. They had enormous, bright eyes, which reflected the
color indigo; their hair was of the golden white light; their
eight-foot-tall bodies were slender, delicate, and lithe.*

*The Yzhnüni resonated most closely to the earth element
of water, for their planet was abundant in it, as are the other*

natural satellites in the Sirian system. In order to hold the Gaian frequency, they were germinated in the highlands of the continent of Atlantis, for there were innumerable caves and grottoes in which they could find the warmth and moisture that best replicated their natural environment, while protecting them from the radiation emitted by the powerful rays of your Solar Deity. It was a terrain that most closely typified the crystalline fields of Yzhnü.

With their first appearance upon the Earth, the Yzhnüni were of such a high vibratory frequency that they could not hold form in the density of your planetary field, nor could they bear any contact with the direct rays emanating from the Sun. To observers, they would have appeared to fade in and out of reality, and they did, indeed, bleed out of the world of matter and back into the sixth dimension repeatedly, until they were finally capable of holding 3D frequency. Their outer sheaths contained none of the pigment required to protect them from the damaging ultraviolet light, and so they were underground in the sunlight hours during those early days of their "distant" migration.

In time, as this Sirian seed took root in three-dimensional reality, their physical beings became denser and more adapted to Earth's geothermal forces and its relationship to the Sun, which once again shone brilliantly through Earth's atmosphere. Their bodies became more solid and resilient, their skin became more opaque, and their coloring took on slightly deeper hues ... a somewhat less translucent quality.

—Atlantis Rising

This portal was a gift from Sirius to the Atlanteans and to all generations of humankind to come, to be utilized at those enormously pivotal times in accelerating human consciousness when the stargates could be opened. Such a time occurred then, when Osiris descended through the gateway from the higher dimensions and into the third, and another such time occurs in short order, when you reach the ascension vortex. Again, it is described in our previous work and we present it to you now:

At a point in the Yzhnüni's earthly evolution, during which time they had effectively trained the novitiates in those practices that would help reestablish the wam frequencies of the natives and the entire ecosystem, the Sirian High Council intervened. We were intent upon accelerating the Atlanteans' understanding of multidimensionality and the higher purpose of humankind's existence, so that they would be able to carry on with the Yzhnüni's work of jump-starting the civilization's collective memory. It would connect them with the infinity of life streaming through the multidimensional body of All That Is.

It was our intention to ensure that the Yzhnüni's presence amongst your great ancestors serve to elevate the mutating starseeded human race from the bondage of survival mind into the pursuit of enlightenment, and to teach the Wisdom to those who would guide the people in that quest. We were directed to help dissolve the grid that had been made to envelop the Earth, so that we could reestablish direct lines of contact with you and with other life forms of your world.

To assist the noble Yzhnüni in their efforts, thirteen crystal skulls of extra-dimensional origins were brought into materialization, "crystallized" in three-dimensional earth frequencies much as you, as soul essences, create the physical bodies in which you reside as 3D beings. Remember that quartz crystals are living beings which record, store, and amplify energy. You have seen this in their practical application in your technology and, although you may not quite understand how it works, you have accepted the use of the silicon chip as the foundation upon which that very technology is built.

Never forget, however, that throughout the universe of matter and permeating the infinite dimensions beyond your current "slice" of reality, the capacity of crystal beings to serve consciousness is exalted when the matrix is activated by directed, focused thought waves of the few and the many. When that focus is set for the highest possible good of the All, magic happens.

As difficult as it might be for you to visualize or to accept, it is quite a simple process bringing crystal beings from an etheric imprint into matter, and this you may have already witnessed in your personal interactions with them. You may have experienced a crystal simply disappearing and then returning to you at another time or place. This is a phenomenon of universal scope and frequency and no, you aren't losing your mind if one of your crystal teachers seems to "disappear into thin air." It is just that the illusions of the world of matter may have you believing that such things cannot happen, just as you may believe that you, too, cannot disappear and return at will. Yet, such occurrences are reported frequently in those lands of ascetics and masters who achieve de-materialization as a result of what you term "mind over matter."

The thirteen skulls brought into manifestation in early Atlantis were "sculpted" as a result of the mind-patterning of higher beings—members of the Family of Light—who were called from many dimensional frameworks to participate in their creation. Delivered unto the earth realm by the Sirian High Council, they were programmed to open the portals of multidimensional awareness to the Yzhnüni ... that they could continue their work with direct access to guidance from the higher dimensions. The thirteen skulls, known to the Family of Light as "the Skull Committee," were stationed in the Temple of Nephthys, deep within an amethyst grotto in the inner earth sanctuary of Yzhnüni worship.

—Atlantis Rising

Osiris, Master of the Golden White Light, came to Earth through the portal opened with the Skull Committee to draw the survivors of second cycle Atlantis out of their sanctuaries within the Earth, so that they might rebuild your world.

A master of light over matter, he was worshipped as the quintessential god of Egypt from which all other records and mythologies spring.

We have much more to share with you, as is appropriate to your discoveries now, of Osiris and the significance of the thirteen crystal skulls of Atlantis.

How does the Committee work together at this point if the Master Skull is not activated as yet?

Each of the skulls of Atlantis, gifted from Sirius, carries the blueprint of **one** of your twelve light strands of DNA—the blueprint of the super race of *Homo sapiens.* Each is a record keeper of the higher dimensional intelligence, which brought it to crystallize in your realm, holding all the frequencies and light forms within it. Is it any wonder to you that they will be reunited at a time when you are reactivating the golden filaments of DNA? The reunion of the twelve, like the rewiring of your twelve strands, activates the Master. Let this serve you as an allegory for your own process.

United, the twelve crystal skulls manifest the original intention of the White Priesthood—that being the opening of the galactic portals at a time that enough of you, the collective mind, would have reached the vibrational frequencies to begin your ascension out of limitation.

When the twelve are united, the Master Skull of Osiris will be "exhumed" from its location and it will take form within the circle of twelve.

In which countries are the skulls located now and are they in the hands of authentic keepers?

That you are hearing so much about the crystal skulls at this time has everything to do with their imminent reunion in the Mayalands, and all that that encompasses for humankind. It is a primordial memory, a part of the collective consciousness of your species.

Many ancient Atlanteans are in body again at this time, having come to rectify the karma that was formed of their thoughts and actions. They hold the memory in their subconscious reservoirs, knowing, at the deepest levels, that the time of reunion is imminent. Indeed, many of these old souls have reincarnated now just to be there, amongst you, when this occurs.

As to the locations of the Atlantean skulls, we can tell you that only three have surfaced in your contemporary reality and that the other nine are in safekeeping, awaiting the time of convergence. The thirteenth, removed altogether from the density of the third dimension, exists in its etheric form below the Osirion in Egypt. It will be materialized at the time the others are joined together.

That so many are enthralled with the vibrational aspects of such modern carvings is, for some, inspired by memory and, for others, it is a projection into a moment when reunion will occur.

You are not the first generation to worship such forms—many others have before you! Ancient carvers have idolized the skull in crystal long before you—so powerful is the memory and the legend of the Skull Committee. Some of these Old World skulls have reappeared now and they have their imprints and codes. Some are incredible light fields, some are of the darkness—for the form of itself is an exceptional container for the storing of information, while the conscious cellular units of the mineral respond to and hold the intention that activated it at any time in its journey.

Others have been created in these, your earth days, and they, too, hold the intent and love of their modern day sculptors. This is why it is so important, when working with such tools, that you clear all energies that are not of the highest intention. It is a mantra that you need if you intend to work with them.

Remember, dear one, that it is all **real:** each experience and the thoughts that emanate from each moment are very real, indeed. It all serves to create the right dynamics for the convergence, for it focuses your minds out of limitation and onto the field of probabilities, which lies just ahead of you, just as it lies within every cell of your being.

What is the role of the Sirian High Council now, in contemporary earth affairs?

We understand your question to be in reference to our interaction with earth beings at this point on the time-space continuum, whose vibration is rising in harmony with the mutating frequencies of your Solar Deity, as he prepares for ascension.

As in other crucial moments in human evolution, wherein your species enjoyed incredible leaps of individual and societal advancement, you are all at the point of reconnection with the galactic family.

This involves, amongst many other things, the arrival of significant numbers of extraterrestrial, three-dimensional beings (from within and beyond your solar system) as well as contact from intelligent extra-dimensional light beings from the higher dimensions.

Some of the extraterrestrials in question will be of the lower vibrations; some will be of the higher. This is the nature of the duality of physical reality, as we have described to you so many times in our works. Some are already well established on the Earth, involved with your governments and their agendas, as we have described to you previously; others are soon to arrive. Some are of the dark persuasion; some of the light; others are somewhere in between.

As to the question of their intention for the interspecies development that will evolve from their interactions with the human race, we remind you that it is the energetic fields of your creative individual and collective thought patterns that will determine how you will receive alien contact ... which will, in turn, determine their natural reactions to you.

The responsibility of the light realms in which we hold resonance is to rekindle within you the knowledge of how you co-create reality with every thought, every word, and every action, serving as a station in mind-space whereby you can receive love and light and dispel fear.

That is our true purpose in making contact with you now, as it has always been across the fields of probability, which you know as the time-space continuum.

This, dear starseed, has been eloquently represented in the pantheon of Egyptian gods, through which your ancestors sought wisdom, guidance, and light from the beyond. Like the ancients, you strive to know what lies beyond the realm of the physical and all that is manifest within your fields of observation.

And, like the Egyptians and other ancient starseed, you are being facilitated to receive the knowledge firsthand, as you evolve with the rising vibrations of Earth.

Was the Great Sphinx a testimony to the beginning of a new era? I ask because I see that usually for a long time the vision of the gods was depicted as a human body with an animal head—and then the Sphinx is an animal body with a human head.

What was the reason for this?

The Great Sphinx, a Sirian effigy, was not originally created with a human head—this transformation was undertaken millennia after its creation and it was a deliberate act intended to feed the ego of the Pharaoh and, in so doing, break the energy.

Even casual observation will reveal to you that the current human-like head is utterly out of proportion with the leonine body, which stares out to the east during certain astrological configurations, across the horizon, at the Sirian star of Sothis.

The Lioness bears witness to ancient starseed, those of early days in the third cycle of Atlantis, who worshipped the sister stars from that point on Gaia's power grid that corresponded with the epicenter of her energy body and the merging of all ley lines within and upon the surface of your planet.

She is the guardian of the fields, holder of the musical scores of Giza which, revealed, will activate the Hall of Records.

I have to ask—what is beneath the Sphinx? We hear for so long about so many different things.

Beneath the Lioness lies the Hall of Records in which are recorded all the thoughts ever thought, all the words ever spoken, and every sacred code ever encoded in the multidimensional Universe.

There are found all the keys to activate the network of pyramids upon all continents, the temples of all worshippers, the energy grids of the outer and inner bodies of Gaia, and access routes to Agharta.

There lies an unadorned chamber, circular in form (representative of the Atum, the One of Creation), which serves as a resonance chamber for the music of Creation to be played when the time is reached that human consciousness can decipher just how the symphony is written and stored in the Sphinx.

Your archeologists have already penetrated this sacred space, disappointed at its simplicity and barren walls, for they have no idea of its purpose. Spiritual masters will be enabled to decode the many layers of consciousness and sound the music and that will only occur when the human race has made the shift, creating the necessary harmonics.

Who will be these master lightworkers who will "activate Giza"? Are you talking about very evolved human beings ... or actual light beings?

Very evolved human beings are light beings. There are many amongst you now, and many more are going to achieve illumination at the time of your emergence—and they will be guided by the Ascended Masters: some of whom you are aware and others, who have yet to rise in your conscious awareness.

Is what is under the Sphinx related to Giza?

It is all interrelated, yes, most certainly. We confirm to you that the Great Pyramid serves many purposes, amongst which it is a chariot in which the Pharaohs enjoyed time travel. From the so-named "sarcophagus" in the king's chamber, they journeyed to many star systems and many dimensions.

Following the principles of simple harmonic motion, wherein multiple frequencies are symmetrical to one point, creating resonance fields, the entire plateau was in harmonic mean proportion to the chamber beneath the Sphinx.

All that is visible to the human eye (the structures that stand above the sands) and all that lies hidden (to all but the elite who secretly explore the below there and at other strategic locations) are harmonically tuned to specific frequencies and musical sequences that can be "played," in a very literal sense, to open the Hall of Records.

It is a slightly oval-shaped space, in the underground, baffling the archeologists for it holds no apparent treasure, bears no inscription, and reveals nothing of its wisdom of humankind's birth and history. All is coded, awaiting the direction of the maestro who can orchestrate the great symphony, which will turn the keys.

There are tunnels all through the below in the area known as the Giza Plateau. These multi-leveled passageways connect the pyramids, the Sphinx, underground cities in their entirety, and burial grounds still rich in history and the material wealth sought out by your modern day conquistadors.

The main passageway, a sacred path into the heart of the Hall of Records, is located between the arms of the Sphinx—just there, behind the breastplate. There only the initiated can pass through the multidimensional doorway for no physical manifestation exists.

For a very long time, I've wanted to ask questions about the Alexandrian Library. I know that it was not an accident when it burned. It occurred because, with the information contained, the scholars could teach the population how to be limitless. When it burned, everything became limited.

At that time, there were many great libraries throughout the world. The Alexandrian Library was situated on a seaport. It seems to have carried a very special energy that had nothing to do with our earth plane. In fact, it came from outside light forces.

It has been said that some documents from the Alexandrian Library were copied or saved and sent to different places on earth. One of those places is the Vatican. When I research this, I've learned that there are over two hundred vaults of archives and each archive may contain over two hundred thousand documents.

Since knowledge is freedom, was the burning of this library a plan from the dark forces to take away all knowledge?

At any moment and at any point in the three-dimensional universe where there exists a power structure or individual whose intention it is to rule over any sentient beings or race, there will also exist a desire to withhold any form of knowledge and wisdom as a fundamental strategy of control.

Domination over another is constructed not only of the whip and sword, for that is so overt in its manifestation that the sublimated can face and potentially overcome the tyrant. Instead, it is the manipulation of consciousness, whereby the individual or society is led away from the light of love and the wonders of universal mind (expressed so eloquently by the ancient luminaries) to wallow in the slowed vibrations of ignorance and darkness that ultimately serve as the key to control and dominate others.

This occurs throughout your history, as it does on other unevolved planets of your dimension, for it is an aspect of the dual nature of your reality. And it is cyclical. You build and burn, raise and level, design and destroy, and then re-create it all—over and over again.

Do bear in mind and soul, however, that in the act of burning the books, what occurred was the imprinting of the Wisdom upon the ethers—where the visions and insights of such enlightened contributors to the human story have been etched upon the Akashic Record. This is the true library of Earth and all is written, from the first thought of Atum, Prime Creator—across the infinite seas of the Cosmos—and from the first atom itself.

Contrary to your statement above: when the library burned, the works were, to a very great extent, **relieved of their limitations** and purified in the flame—to be imprinted, in a higher form, in the ethers.

If this library was under the guidance of the light forces, then why was it permitted that so much of the history of Earth, teachings, and information be burned?

Everything is God, Prime Creator, the Seed Thought. All springs from that Divine Will, the Goodness, the Essence, the Source and so it is that everything that occurs in the illusion in which you reside is but a playing out of cause and effect, darkness to light ... infinitely, eloquently, and with profound experience and wisdom, rising from the dance of opposition and harmony.

There have been so many Dark Ages in your history. Atlantis, Lemuria, Alexandria, the Crusades, and even now—your contemporary earth societies are at the destruction point—appearing to careen towards your own annihilation. You know, however, that, like the phoenix, you always arise, resurrecting yourselves from the ignorance that drives you to the extremes: back in flight, towards the light. You call these periods "eras of rebirth," and with each you rise higher than the epoch that led you there.

We ask you to consider that, as such, the darkness of such moments and their violent acts (to which the collective nonetheless contributes through its passivity and materialism) is as much a part of the light that rebounds from the gloomy caves of the collective unconscious as is the brilliance of resurrection itself.

Can we retrieve this knowledge from the guidance realm?

Yes, indeed, you do have the capabilities now to retrieve all wisdom from the Akashic Record, for you are fast remembering that you are multidimensional beings, created in the mind of Prime Creator, a spark of the Eternal Light.

Much of the library of scrolls is so utterly antiquated that, given an opportunity to return to that place on the time-space continuum that preceded the burning, you might just find the anticipation far exceeded the experience.

We urge you to forgive the past injustices and to understand how they serve you and then concentrate your mind and heart upon the very now of your existence, for you are alive in one of the most revealing of all eras of history: the dawn of your Sun's ascension.

Soon you will be able to read the scrolls of countless ancient sages and the holograms of those who appear beyond you in the matrix of human experience, right there, from the comfort of your armchairs upon eternity—activated to see what, for most, has been hidden.

You are passing out of the Dark Age of contemporary repression and ignorance, dear one, into the Light of the Forever Fields.

Will the Vatican ever release some of this information?

It is doubtful. With all its links to the secret societies and power brokers of the Earth, the power network that rules over you, it is designed to hold you in obedience. Why, then, would its rulers provide you with the knowledge that would release you from their hold over such a vast part of your contemporary societies, especially now—as they push forward the agenda of another of their so-named "holy wars"?

Holy war? How irreverent an utterance!

No, indeed, as long as the power brokers remain upon their gilded thrones they will hold on to what they believe is theirs to hold from you: the lost scrolls of enlightenment. They have raped the great libraries, defaced and hidden the codes, and putrefied the wells of pure vision, because they believe themselves (privileged members of the ruling elite) in every way superior to you, the "masses."

They believe that, as a body of beings to be controlled and made subservient, you are more easily restrained when you are herded into the corrals of ignorance and blind obedience. And so they cling hard and fast to those tattered pages of past masters, many of whom were true visionaries, working for the light, and others—who were not.

Let this not surprise you. Many of those intellectual masters of the past explored the mysteries of ancient worlds—their technologies, sciences, and records of galactic events—in order to manipulate form and vibration to alter the power grids of global rule. Of these, significant numbers were enslaved to the dark forces of control on your planet, and their intentions were of the lowest vibration. These secrets—elaborated by those of the dark intent—are being used today as they were then.

Others, the light bringers, were guided to help lift humankind out of the deep valleys of repression and onto the mountaintops of illumination. And here again, the wisdom of those light ones of old is being retrieved by those lightworkers of your era who come to the information with the light intent ... and that focus is manifesting with the raising of human consciousness.

Remember, however, that we have told you in our works that you would first pass through the Desert Days on your way to the dawn and that is where you are now.

Once you remember that the overriding experience of the reality in which you hold residence is the existence of duality at all levels, you will understand that every action does indeed hold an equal and opposite reaction and that, in the great scheme of things in the Cosmic Order, it all eventually reaches resolution.

When you have mastered simplicity of thought and mind, you will recognize that the great scholars devoted their lifetimes to exploring the wonders of Creation and the perfection of exis-

tence. Upon these observations they traveled the roads of intellect and contemplation to bring you their works.

We invite you always to remember that their most complex
observations are found everywhere in nature and these same principles are there for you to uncover with your own eyes: the cosmometry of life, the form, the color, the vibration. All the wisdom
that you believe "lost" lies before your very eyes, within reach: in
the petals of a rose; as the colors of the sky across the spectrum
of Earth's revolutions; from the magnificence of your own incredible form.

Is it an energy of fear?

We experience ignorance and fear as interchangeable and believe
that any time one soul intends power over another it is essentially
an act of ignorance of one's godliness (however dim the spark
shines within), just as it is a manifestation of that same individual's
fascination with the lowest sensory vibrations that come with the
first leap into the abyss into which new souls leap from Source.

Inherent in the worship of darkness is the fear that one will
never reach the light and that there is far more safety in controlling a loveless reality of false mastery and worship than there is in
surrendering, egoless, to the Light.

Will we have to wait until after 2012 for these vaults to be open?

Dear one, the vaults **are** opening! You are the turners of the pages
of ancient texts, once you understand that you contain all the wisdom of the Universe in every cell of your memory and that the

Akashic Record lies just as much within you as it does in the ethers.

As you evolve into higher states of consciousness, you begin to pull this universal wisdom out of the waters of your ancestral wells—your subconscious—and into the stream of contemporary thought. Remember that all that was written was burned into the ethers: it is but a reflection of The All That Is, That Ever Was, and That Always Will Be. Much of it you have already learned; some you are discovering has not been lost, such as the sculpted record; more is being healed at the etheric level so that it can progress into the higher realms and find the light of higher consciousness.

If there are archives in the Vatican, surely there are others elsewhere. Would there be some under the pyramids? I heard that some are also in France, Tibet, under the sands of Baghdad, even in the United States there are some ... is that so?

These libraries are not only textual, you do understand. Wherever humankind faced prosecution for free thought, it was most often necessary to bury the profound revelations in code, contained within the hidden scriptures of the greatest written texts of your present awareness: the Bible, the Koran, the Torah, and all books of ancient religions. All are coded.

Our own messages are coded with multiple layers of consciousness, energy, and vibration. This is not a difficult process to achieve once you have mastered the intricacies of multidimensional communication.

These libraries you so mourn are often right in front of you—

in great artworks, in architecture, in nature's own design. And, again we remind you that the books you so long for are merely interpretations of those essential universal properties of God, life, and your existence both as sparks of Creation and as units of self-awareness within those frameworks.

Trust us. The actual physical libraries of old have been outdated by the laboratories and universities of modern earth societies, just as they have been raised even further in conscious application within your spiritual circles of light and Gaia's radiant fields.

I read also that there are places in the Vatican where humans cannot walk. What kind of energy is in that place to produce such a thing? If so, what is the purpose of this energy? Are they afraid of what we would discover in these vaults?

Yes, this is true but it is nothing more than an energy force field creating a shield of protection against entry into the secret vaults. It is similar to the Vril Power that guards the entry points into the inner world of Agharta, although it is far less complex than that which is needed to seal the tunnels into the sacred world that lies within Gaia.

The Vril force described in some of your earlier texts is created by the manipulation of gravitation forces to such an extent that, applied, they can disassemble the cellular makeup of any biological life form that happens into it.

This force, one of the oldest technologies of humankind, has been harnessed by the power elite and is used in many applications on Earth and in space. Although they have yet to master it, they do know far more than you are privileged to and much of this information has come from the texts of old just as it has been gifted from aliens friendly with your governments.

8

Sacred Sites, Celestial Messages

Sites of worship are pulsating with the energies of angelic beings, elemental spirits, interplanetary councils, many initiates, adepts, and masters, and you will feel the power of group soul when you join together in worship.

You can feel the spirits of the light congregating, focusing consciousness at the sites, and this is part of your attraction there. As you dance across the junctures in the starlight days of great transformation, you are weaving the Gossamer Web, reuniting with the Mother. Hasten, for you must accomplish a great deal from now until the closing of time and, by taking yourselves to her power, you are committing your conscious acknowledgment of Gaia, while fusing with other light beings who, like you, are coming home—speeding up your process by leaps and bounds.

The nine centers of Earth's primary energy network are: the Giza Plateau, Mt. Kailash in Tibet, the England Triangulation (Avebury–Glastonbury–Stonehenge), Brittany, the Peruvian Andes, Mt. Shasta in California, the Pyramid Valley of Tenochtitlan in Mexico, Oahu in Hawaii, and the Native American energy wheels of New Mexico. The secondary sites include Ayers Rock in Australia, Damascus in Syria, certain vortex points in Siberia (still to be investigated), Mt. Sinai in Israel, Easter Island, and Native American energy wheels in Mexico, Guatemala, and the

United States. You must travel far, overcoming many obstacles, but that is the nature of initiation and most of you, the awakening, have already set off upon your journeys. The time is upon you and there is no turning back and so, go now, and spread the light.

The Cosmos of Soul

You call us to visit the sacred sites indicated in Cosmos of Soul. Some of these, such as the Giza Plateau in Egypt and the temples of the Maya, are well frequented by spiritual travelers, and others are relatively unknown as sacred sites. What are your criteria for determining these locations?

Dear one, it is not we who determine where the incredible vibrational peaks lie in your world: the musical keyboard of the Gaian wave. It is the worship of ancients, who have constructed their mighty icons, and others, who have always listened to the pulse of Gaia in the trees and rivers, passing the knowledge from father to son, from mother to daughter; it is the spirit beings, who hold the patterns of consciousness there; it is the music of Gaia, ringing out from her vibrational epicenters, calling you home.

These, all of these, are determined by Gaia's own electromagnetic energy body, for it is at those points of the highest vibrations that sacred sites exist in nature and have been immortalized by ancients.

I believe that I have evolved to a point where I can tune in to the energies without having to physically bring myself to these locations. Therefore, I am not sure I agree with your message that it is so important for us to enter these spaces.

Ours is a call for you to acquire the data, the vibrational codes, the imprinted etheric waves, and powerful emotional energies that are available to you at the chakric centers—the sacred sites—of your planet, once you are able to unlock the codes that protect such spaces and enter there as Initiates to the mysteries.

With each experience, an epiphany of the soul will mark your journey. With the retrieval of the veiled comes the unveiling.

Such processes at this pivotal moment in your wild ride upon Planet Earth serve to bring you to the absolute center of your being. It is from there that you are achieving the ability to read the knowledge your "future" self holds in the ethers, to decipher the Wisdom left by those who have long ago passed along the spiral of light, and to fine-tune your understanding of other dimensional realities.

This you need now in order to proceed with your personal vision quest, helping you to remember your soul mission.

Remember, too, that you bring light, wisdom, and joy to the power places, and these waves of higher consciousness are exalted in the vibrations, reflected in and imprinted upon the ethers.

These energies, this focus, are of the utmost importance at this time.

We understand, from our collective and individual experiences, that this is the way of the Initiate of the third density realms, such as yours, and so we invite you to partake of the wealth that is your heritage in the sacred fields, the high mountains, and the streams. More importantly, we invite you to share it, through your heartsong, to the others—whether they join you there, or whether they receive the waves from afar.

Let us be clear. If you are capable of receiving those wonders by reaching attunement on other levels, then blessed are you indeed. Never do we suggest that there is only one way—a right way—to travel the pathways of soul seeking higher ground.

Perhaps you are achieving mastery of your earthly existence at this stage in your journey and, if so, we celebrate your achievements.

One cautionary word to your heart from ours, dear one: beware of the ego, which will shut you down every time.

Beware of the ego self.

Please elaborate for us how these sacred sites are activated and describe to us the mechanics of their astral and interdimensional attraction.

Those locations referred to as "sacred sites" by the many who are in tune now and from the times of the ancients are the neurological tuning forks for Gaia. These spots are to the Earth Mother as your pulse points are to you: here are reflected the currents and electromagnetic charges, the flow lines, of her immense physical, mental, emotional, and astral bodies.

Beings from many dimensions are attracted to experience these incredible reservoirs and fountains of celestial flow as are human beings, from times of the ancients to your contemporary worshippers, indigenous peoples and those, like you, who have begun their pilgrimage to the sites of power.

Like iron filings to the magnet, clustering at the poles, so are higher astral beings pulled to these vortices of the Earth as well as other celestial bodies in your realm. There they are energized by the force fields of Gaia, but more—they are bathed in the light of those who meditate, pray, celebrate, and take initiation at the points of Earth's highest charge.

With the acceleration now occurring in Gaia's fields, the power points serve as gateways to merging dimensions. Visiting there, your hearts open to the potential of all consciousness to imprint the ethers, and you will find an infinity of remarkable experiences are yours to behold and make sacred within you.

Are the myriad three-dimensional extraterrestrials now entering earth space also attracted to these locations?

Yes. They are not only attracted to the power points, they are actually facilitated by their energy output. The highly charged energy tubes that extend from these locations out, through earth atmosphere (Gaia's aura) and beyond, to the space just beyond the magnetosphere, serve as magnetic force fields which assist them in navigating their way through your complex grids and into earth space.

Understanding what we have told you about the laws of resonance and magnetic attraction, you can well imagine how the consciousness inherent in such emanations directly and indirectly affects who (or what) is drawn to these vortices on all levels.

So, by visiting the sites and doing our spirit work there, are we actually calling these extraterrestrial navigators to us?

Yes, indeed, you are doing just that. This is why it is of the utmost importance that you go there with open hearts, centered in humility and reverence and focused upon the highest intention: the good of the All. It is every bit as important to the creation of the moment of contact as will be the moment itself.

Your presence and your prayers accelerate the "time" line of this episode in the book of galactic affairs and help to determine the outcome of that first wave of visitations, when humankind is finally confronted with what, until now, has always appeared to you as an extraordinary "possible reality."

You are sending the message of love and acceptance out through those very energy tubes that form the magnetic fields for the craft; you are amongst the primary representatives of a peaceful Earth—the galactic family of Gaia.

Your prayers, meditations, toning, and celebration are experienced in the waves, just as many of you are actually being observed there, as craft continually fly overhead.

These are often shielded from observation; other times they are in plain view.

Be aware of all that surrounds you.

Your reference to "energy wheels" in the Americas is vague and I am curious to know more precisely what areas you are referring to in that text.

We speak of vast energy vortices found in the caverns, lakes, and plains of the continent of the Americas North. These vital Gaian force fields are guarded by the true Earth Keepers and cannot be revealed to you at this time, for they are vulnerable to exploitation by those of the dark persuasion ... as every attempt is made to break the power of the indigenous peoples, guardians of the earth temples.

We can tell you, however, that they are lock-on points for future interplanetary alignments, when your Earth and the family of planetary deities move through the astral cords of your Sun.

In a most amazing spiritual quest with your channel, Patricia Cori, through the mystery lands of Egypt, we entered the Great Pyramid to activate the third strand of DNA. There, in an intensely rich experience of group toning, most of us heard Tibetan monks chanting with us—in the ethers.

Can you elaborate on this phenomenon and speak to how sound is woven through the energy vortices of Gaia?

The common experience of all evolved civilizations in the light realms of the multidimensional Universe is the understanding of sound as the weaver of all frequencies. It is thought, crystallizing to a slower frequency at select points of time and space, and then creating a lattice, or pattern, that moves all souls forward, upon the Great Spiral of our return to Source.

This we have previously referred to as the "Music of the Spheres," for all consciousness resounds as music in the infinite Cosmos of Soul: from the minutiae of subatomic particles to the vastness of planetary beings, solar deities, and yes, entire galaxies and then universes ... and then beyond, for the Cosmos is infinite in ways that are unfathomable to the human mind.

Masters of sound and its profound relevance, the Tibetans have long worked to hold the music of Gaia in perfect balance. Just like trained tuners of instruments, they are intent upon assisting Gaia in maintaining her perfect pitch, the music of her soul. From the ancients of Atlantis and Lemuria, to the Priesthood of Egypt, the Maya ... all understood the significance of music and vibration to the emotional balance of Gaia.

Before humankind disturbed and now destroys the song of the seas—the rhythms and melodies of the Great Whales and the Dolphin Beings—the primordial notes of Earth were crystalline and pure.

Before the blight of your waste and destruction, the bird call, the rush of the forest stream, even the hiss of the reptilians ... all were harmonious: all was in perfection in the Garden of Eden.

You could hear the heartbeat of the Great Mother resounding through the earth and you could feel the waves of her vital pulse through the secondary chakric centers, located in the soles of your feet.

This perfect balance of sound and vibration still exists at all the power points of Gaia and the enlightened know how to travel there, on the winds of directed vocal or instrumental sounds.

They are capable of remotely retrieving the new information—your group intention—in these vortices, just as they are able to receive the pulse of what vibrates there. And yes, they do also send their love there to facilitate your experience, joining with you in the celebration of your discovery and attuning, in a sense, to the intention of your group soul, reaching higher.

Your being there, in full awareness, calls them to take part in the fine-tuning of earth energies. It is the prayer of all ages—of all the living of Gaia—and you are privileged to be there: to bring your love light to these places and to hear and feel the love shining back to you.

There are also key lightworkers on the planet who understand how to unlock the codes and retrieve the information that has been encoded for the initiations of many at different times and places on the Great Planet Earth.

I have journeyed to Egypt recently and have been disturbed to see that the government there is building a high wall and gates around the Giza Plateau. They claim it is to protect the monuments.

Can you tell us what is the real reason they are blocking these gifts to humanity from our view?

As we have elaborated for you in our work *Atlantis Rising,* those in power on your planet are determined to bring Gaia's fields to the lowest possible frequencies, in an attempt to create resonance with Nebiru and drag the planet through with you.

Your prayers, meditations, and energy work within the sacred sites, particularly the Great Octahedron, raise the vibration, activating the grids, changing the musical octaves.

They do not want you there. This is the reason for the destruction of the energies of Tibet, the enclosures of the Giza stargates, closure of Mayan sacred sites, and continual interference in the affairs of the indigenous peoples, who still hold secret those sacred energy wheels in their lands.

This is why it is so important that you go there, in your circles of light, illuminating Gaia's electromagnetic energy lines and activating the chakric wheels of the Earth.

Do not be deterred. No walls, nor gates, nor armed guards can stop you.

Go to the sacred sites now, daringly and with great purpose, and you will open what needs to be opened, sending the love light through to the very "fingertips" of Gaia's immense body.

I dream of opening direct communication with you, of the Sirian High Council, or with other multidimensional light beings like you. Are you also drawn to the sacred sites of Earth? Is it more likely that I can personally experience your presence there?

Yes, indeed. We are drawn to those points on the space-time continuum where we find resonant frequencies, and this attunement is accelerated at the great vortices of Gaia, just as we are drawn into your circles of light—now proliferating around the globe.

We resonate very strongly with the pyramid grid lines of Earth. You may or may not be aware that pyramid forms are surfacing and being discovered in locations around the planet. This has everything to do with the activation of Giza at the millennium and the process you are now experiencing as the evolution of your planet.

The Great Octahedron of Giza is the master switch: the key to all the electromagnetic energy lines of Gaia.

More pyramid structures will be unearthed soon as the mysteries are revealed. They have been activated on the grid lines and are bringing themselves into the light of human consciousness!

We hover, as orbs of light, in those sacred halls and fields, sharing in your wonder and excitement as you bring your light and love into the kaleidoscope of energies that weave the colors of all that is sacred and profound.

Just as we located and made contact with our channel at the crop circles, so do we await you and journey with you through the high energy fields of the sacred power points of Gaia.

Can you speak about the controversy over the crop circles? There have been so many documentaries about how they are made and these are very convincing in proving they are of human design.

The universal language—that which permeates all dimensions, all realities, all conscious realms—is cosmometry: the organization of thought-directed waves of energy into vibratory sequences that manifest in harmonic proportions, defining the true order that exists within chaos.

It is the vehicle upon which intelligence communicates and therefore it is exciting to those of us who imprint these forms upon the wheat fields (and other hospitable environments) to see the response of human glyph creators appear, alongside those of extra-dimensional origin.

The sheer will and focus of these talented earth mathematicians and artistic technicians to deny any other explanation but theirs we find endearing, in that they are driven to respond to our galactic artworks with their rudimentary and yet sufficient means of attempted reproductions.

We do recognize and appreciate how their works do also have a certain energy about them.

This is communication and we are speaking to each other just as was intended! You cannot but enjoy the cosmic humor in the fact that on the one hand, they deny our existence and yet, on the other, they reply to our messages.

They speak our language and teach us so much about the nature of the human psyche—on individual and collective levels. They teach us about humankind's desire and your amazing capacity to alter and transmute social consciousness.

As for discerning which of the myriad glyphs is of the other-worldly nature and which is fruit of skeptics of the human variety—we can only tell you that this Truth you will find within.

There is a vibratory signature in those formations that we and other star beings create for you that is not present in those of the human hand. Each is a powerful interstellar vortex—a point of conscious interdimensional connection—and we do believe you will experience the shift in energy that defines that sacred space, where the intent of light beings from other realms takes form as architectural mathematics: sacred geometry.

Those produced by the doubting mechanics do not resonate nor do they glisten in the light of the soaring spirit of humankind.

Go to the fields to feel, firsthand, the waves of light passing over and through you.

Find your own Truth, allowing no individual, no campaign, no evidence to stand between you and your inner knowing: your spiritual experience.

Now is the time for you to take nothing **but** Truth as "given" while remaining open to the infinite possibilities of all that lies within your reach.

In 2006 there were far fewer formations than years past. What is happening? Are you abandoning this method of communication?

The penetrating heat waves that bore down upon the regions where we concentrate our designs evaporated substantial quantities of the watershed that lies below the earth surface.

We interact with the consciousness of water element as a conductive electromagnetic field, which holds the design as a blueprint from below, while we create the energy fields from above.

Our scientists have recently photographed a perfect hexagonal form at Saturn's north pole. Can you share your insights into what has created this configuration?

As you come closer to understanding the relatedness of all conscious beings in the Cosmos, reaching beyond the constraints of earthly realities, you begin to understand that the ultimate communication of intelligence—Creation itself—is mathematical and that within the structural perfection of mathematics is formed the cosmometry of all existence.

That breathtaking formation upon that planet speaks of the wisdom of that cosmic being and the vibration it will be holding as it prepares to pass alongside of you, through the exquisite cord of solar light.

You, who have a spiritual sense of number and form, will recognize that within the hexagonal form is embedded the axiom: As Above, So Below and As Below, So Above.

Do you see, dear ones, how the messages laid down in your crop formations are representative of the universal language of consciousness?

I find it hard to understand why Tibet, a holy land of such spiritual dedication to the course of humanity, has been slowly destroyed and the spirit of these noble people broken.

What insights do you have for us with regard to the injustice perpetrated against the spiritual leaders and the innocent of this land?

One of the greatest lessons of our individual and collective experience lies in learning to embrace the impermanence of all things—the eternal "becoming" of all that exists in the Universe.

At the same time, it is the most difficult, perhaps, as we cling so desperately to the illusion of our existence in the material realm and so resist change in our passing through the various phases of our lifetimes upon the great wheel of karmic return.

No greater teachers are there now in your midst to show you the meaning of "letting go" than the Tibetan masters themselves, who have now descended from the mountaintops to bring you the beauty of the lesson—a lesson they have lived to tell.

Life, you are learning, is like the brightly colored sands of the mandala: now shining the intricate wisdom of the ancients upon the temple floor; now the colorful bits of an ancient puzzle, scattered about by the first evening wind.

The closing of the Tibetan portal occurs at a time when humanity is ready to receive the teachings that, for so long, have lain secreted away in the silence of monastic isolation.

This is the blessing that you can glean from the Tibetan story, once you change your focus to contemplate the significance of what the Tibetan masters bring to you, rather than mourning what they have had to leave behind.

It has been brought to my attention that the Mother /Father Crystals of Atlantis are currently powering up just off the coast of Florida where I live and Atlantis is preparing to take on more energy and rise from the ocean—quite soon for all to see, in order to speed up the ascension process more rapidly. I have also heard of amazing finds off the coast of Cuba.

Can you expand on this information?

In these underwater regions now being discovered in the locations of the Caribbean Sea, there are indeed exciting developments triggering the mineral mind of Gaia and they are naturally sparking your intelligence, your curiosity, and your memory.

All along the great continental land mass of ancient Atlantis, which reached from the icy seas of the northern earth pole to the southern ports of your existing land mass of South America, lie untold treasures of your past, awaiting discovery.

Within the next five years of your calendar, you will witness one after another after another of the ancient cities of Atlantis and Lemuria (in the region of Southern Pacific seas) begin to emerge, rising from the ocean depths, breaking through, where until now they lay hidden below the ice ... just as they are rising from the deep subconscious memory of your collective experience.

The crystal body of Gaia is Earth's Akashic library: holding all knowledge, all history, and all experience of what transpires in the earth realm. The entire crystalline form of Earth can be and has been activated by the processes of planetary evolution, biological development, and the perpetual interaction of the planet with the other celestial bodies and intergalactic forces with which it shares environment, space, and experience.

The mineral world serves as the electromagnetic resonance board of the entire planet and it stores, generates, and reflects electromagnetic energy throughout every aspect of its being.

It holds the records for those crystal keepers who are called to access the vast library of your planet: upon the surface, within the caves, and below the seas.

Crystal generators that rise as high as trees now become available to you and discoveries abound. The thirteen crystal skulls will soon be united and this will open all the stargates, as parallel universes collide—and all that is new is birthed in the vesica piscis formed at the intersection.

If you are paying attention now, you know that the lies are unraveling, the secrets are being revealed, and Atlantis—land of primordial man—is rising.

In Atlantis Rising you describe the Committee of Thirteen Crystal Skulls and their significance to human evolution. What is the link between the thirteen ancient crystal skulls and the light beings of Sirius?

Twelve skulls were gifted to you, the human race, at the time of the first cycle of Atlantis by Pleiadian and Sirian Light Emissaries. The thirteenth, which we have referred to as the "Master," materialized at the union of the twelve. All were united in the Temple of Nephthys, at that quadrant of the great Atlantean continent which now lies underwater: the so-named Devil's Triangle, specifically off the coast of the location you know as Bimini.

The original twelve were later given to carefully chosen guardians of the White Brotherhood to be carried to safe locations at key energy centers around the globe, while the thirteenth de-materialized back into its etheric imprint, awaiting the reunion.

What can you tell us about the crystal skulls and the Mayan prophecy that they will be reunited in 2012?

We concur that the winter solstice 2012 will be the time of reunion for the Skull Committee. The Mayans will coordinate the alignments of time, space, and location and all will be called together, as was determined from the time of the ancient Atlantean Priesthood.

This "homecoming" is well under way. Currently, seven of the thirteen have come out of hiding and are known to the Mayan leadership. The others, still protected, will emerge in these hours of earth evolution.

Together with their Guardians, they will be called to the Primary Stargate, in the Mayan territories, for the opening of all ascension portals on Earth. This powerful conclave of energies will be charged by the intense solar waves that will mark the celestial "kundalini rising" climax of your Sun, as he readies for ascension.

Are you suggesting that, at that time, ascension of masses of people will occur and if so, are there specific locations, relating to the sacred sites, which will be most significant to this process?

We are stating that the first wave will depart and others will follow when the planet moves through. December 21, 2012, is merely a marker on the time-space continuum, representing the closing down of artificial time and the embracing of a new paradigm as you prepare to become fully aware, galactic beings.

In the first wave of ascension, when those of you who will serve as sentinels and leaders will depart ahead of the others, the portals and gateways will open for you at key sites on the planetary grid lines—and these you no doubt recognize as the sacred sites in Egypt, the Americas, and Peru.

Do you have anything else you want to say to us with regard to our imminent passage and the experience we all must face as we make this transition? We look to you for guidance, comfort, and hope.

We ask you always to remember that Spirit, the all-encompassing force that surrounds, penetrates, and creates every living thing, drives life forward: from seed to tree; from the obscure to the crystalline; from ignorance to knowledge; from the darkness into the light.

So do we, sparks of divine grace, strive to achieve illumination, however long our process.

Do not be deceived by appearances, there where, for so many, it seems that only darkness reigns.

Reflections of an infinite spectrum of light, your appearance in this physical realm is but a brief passage on your timeless journey. What you came to learn as you travel the road home determines just how long you want to linger in the shadows and that is something, we have told you time and time again, that you decided well before you were birthed into this lifetime ... that body ... your world.

As members of the galactic family, our true purpose, often disguised in the illusions of material reality or sabotaged by the conditions of our lives, is to shine the light out to the other, to walk in the grace of our godliness, to give power and strength to all the living, and to live in the light of love.

"Letting God" (however perceived at the conscious level)

through you is the greatest miracle of being human, for in experiencing the divinity of your being—the Highest Self—you express the reason for your existence. You discover your purpose. You serve the greater good.

Just as you worship God, the Great Mathematician, as Creator of the Universe, so must you honor your part as co-creator of all reality ... and so must you strive and intend that the highest purpose always be served.

Letting God through your hearts, minds, and hands, you serve Spirit in its highest aspect.

Let there be no mistake about it ... that is what gives meaning to your existence and it is the only thing that makes sense of the human condition. You heal and are healed, love and are loved ... raising the vibration, as lightworkers of Planet Earth and children of the Universe.

You know that enormous changes in your individual and collective consciousness are needed and that the time is upon you. You feel it—we experience your sensitivity to the reality that lying just beyond the gloomy shadows is a clearing, where Light shines eternal, no longer obscured from your vision ... not even for a moment.

You are beginning to realize that it is, indeed, time to let go of fear and limitation, so that you can truly release yourselves from the grip they hold upon your spirit, sabotaging your happiness and peace of mind.

You are ready for the process of healing to succeed and reach completion and the ecstasy to begin.

You are awakening, starseed.

You need only take a few steps more upon the stairway of light and you will be bathed in the heartlight of those who have passed before you.

There you will catch a glimpse of us, just ahead of you, clearing the way ... to the stars.

9

Final Thoughts

For Trydjya—the Channel of the Sirian High Council: The purpose of your work today

Could you describe the work that you were called to do in Egypt in this last journey?

In these years since my first clear contact from the Sirian High Council, I (like so many of us) have been thrown about on the path of Spirit, tested, challenged, and rewarded as the search for knowledge has guided me to the sacred sites of the Earth. There, as the Council explains to us, are encoded the teachings of the ancient sages and these are most often located at the highest vibration vortices we find in power points of the planet.

In the case of this particular journey to Egypt, for which I was told I would be asked to connect into the absolute heart center of this land, Abydos, I have been guided to travel into the underworld below the great Osirion in order to receive the stores of galactic information that are encoded in the mineral realms below. This message was given me by the Sirian High Council, who are guiding me to and through all the sacred sites and holy temples of this earth in these very powerful years of my life—as a student of Spirit and guide to others.

There I was shown what I believe is one of the greatest secrets yet to be retrieved and it is very exciting to bring it forward in these days of discovery, as it links so many things together and helps me understand, at a very personal level, what is happening now.

I make no claim of its importance to others, since it is such a subjective experience. I merely bring forward my own experience to be shared, trusting that it will serve the greater good. It will be elaborated in my work in progress—*Where Pharaohs Dwell*—which will be released shortly.

Below the magnificent Temple of Sety I in Abydos lies the Osirion, a megalithic structure that has yet to be understood by archeologists, for it truly doesn't seem to fit in any established time frame of dynastic Egypt. To date, no known researcher or Egyptologist has been able to identify its purpose, explain its design, or postulate its significance. It remains, for all intents and purposes, an enigma.

It has been compared to the stone structure of the Temple of the Sun in Peru, for its strangely cut corner megalithic pillars, which appear in that civilization—but not in Egypt.

Although in the past it was possible to enter into the Osirion, today it is forbidden by the Department of Antiquities, given the fact that the entrance and inner rooms are swamped with stagnant, putrid waters too deep to wade through—or at least that is the reason given.

From what I have seen in this experience, both from a physical experience and an astral journey into the depths of the structure, I believe we are about to discover one of the most important aspects of our past and future here.

Final Thoughts

What kind of ritual did you do in the Osirion?

As always, doors open for me in most miraculous ways. I was given the opportunity to spend private time in the grounds of the Osirion without a soul around me other than the true temple guardian, Amir, who held the space for me at all times during my ritual work in Osirion and in the glorious Temple of Sety I.

I am blessed to be the guardian of a magnificent Mayan crystalline skull, Estrella, which was gifted to me during a ritual in Palenque in 2005, during which time I brought a SoulQuest™ Journeys group to the sacred sites of the Maya. Since receiving it from the Mayan Shaman, Kayun, I have been guided to bring it with me to every ceremony, in every site, that I am conducting in these years of discovery and spiritual journeying.

The most important of the rituals I performed in the Osirion was to place the crystal skull into the murky waters for purification. This was not an easy task as the water is deep and the skull could easily have fallen out of reach, so I had to hold on to it while going into the altered state of consciousness.

Then, too, I had to overcome my own discomfort over the appearance of the water, which is a cesspool of pollution, waste, and slime, and raise my consciousness to understand that the water is **sacred**. I had to override the illusion of appearances and embrace the higher understanding of the waters and this, of itself, was an aspect of the Initiation.

I was guided that my feet and hands would have to be in the water as well and this too I followed, with difficulty, knowing that the energies of this holy place would nonetheless hold the water sacred, despite the appearance it held.

I held Estrella in the waters of the Osirion, my feet dangling there as well. My physical sight clouded over, opening the way for third-eye visions.

The skull began to speak, as she has on other occasions.

> *Beneath these waters lies a secret that you are invited to bring back to the world. Peer into the well, center yourself in humility, and fear not. You are surrounded in the Golden White Light of Osiris, Master of the light realms of Sirius.*
>
> *Of the thirteen crystal skulls of Atlantis, which we have described to you as "the Skull Committee," the Master lies in the deep earth below this temple: the burial place of the Osirian effigy—the gateway to the Halls of Amenti.*
>
> *It is the thirteenth of those crystal skulls that were gifted to humankind during the time of Atlantis that lies buried here, its etheric blueprint contained within a protective shield, where also is found the DNA of the Sirian Master, Osiris.*
>
> *Look deep, starseed, deeper than you have ever looked before.*
>
> *Guided by the Council of Sirian Light, you have been asked here to unveil the secrets and discover the true road to Amenti. You will have been initiated when you have brought our experience to the Mayalands—where preparations are being made to reunite the Atlantean skulls.*
>
> *You will be challenged, obstructed, and deterred. It is not new to you; however, this will be your greatest challenge.*
>
> *This is the way of the Spirit Warrior. You move forward, egoless, in service to the All.*

*Always remember, starseed, your path is illuminated
and you know how to shield yourself from the dark force
just as you know when to shine the light of Truth into the
shadows.*

The journey of soul purification that followed that announce-
ment, and my visions as I passed through the underworld below
the Osirion, have been monumental for me and I am still decoding the experience. Moreover, I am still working through the
process, trying to decipher the meaning to my personal life and the
significance, if any, that it holds for others.

What is the purpose of this initiation and how is it related to today?

In the process of passing tests and the endless initiations we undertake as soul moving higher, we are not always privileged to know
the purpose of every step we take on the long road of return.
What I do glean from these very intense experiences is, on many
levels, very personal. It requires much introspection to learn, as a
student of Spirit, what their purpose is to my soul's progression
and how it all serves the highest good.

We are asked to listen to the guidance, follow our hearts, and
take the leaps of faith that often seem so insurmountable, dangerous, and devoid of logic. It requires letting go of the fear of
judgment and criticism and above all else, holding the ego at bay.

I have learned in my work with the Council to try, as best I
can, to silence the left brain—the voice of logical thought—and
follow the intuition to become as receptive as possible to ener-

gies, thought patterns, and vibrations as I can. This, then, I reflect back in every way possible, to those with whom I interact—either energetically or through the word.

In the desire to remain in humility before the wondrous events that unfold around me, I can merely state that I have had a monumental experience. I know that it will be disregarded by many who deny anything other than the so-called "scientific proof," but nonetheless I will move forward with the information that was given me and I will go to the Mayan shamans with the encoded skull, Estrella, trusting that it will be received with open hearts and minds.

We will need to wait to see what unfolds as we pass the time marker of December 21, 2012.

Nonetheless, I believe that the unification of the thirteen crystal skulls will be facilitated by our collective understanding of the meaning of the resurrection of Osiris (when the thirteen pieces are reunited to birth Horus) and that our ability to understand this metaphor will facilitate the activation of the crystal skulls. This is our collective experience, not a personal one. The joy is understanding how it all fits together and being egoless in whatever role I or anyone else will play in that moment.

It is so important to be in surrender and service.

What will happen when they are reunited, in your opinion?

That wealth of information, the Earth Record, will be available to us all and with the opening and merging of the gateways we will be free to journey the galactic highway. We will see the entirety of it all—the workings of the physical universe and beyond, and we will realize the Atum.

What do you understand the Council to mean when they speak of "realizing the Atum"?

I understand the metaphor to be telling us that the physical universe in which we reside is but a single atom—like Atum, lord of Creation—and that it is merely a microcosmic speck upon the infinity of all consciousness. Once we understand that, as sparks of the Godlight, we are eternal, infinite, and unlimited, we will throw off the shackles of our limitation and reach illumination—realizing the Atum.

How did you know that you would have this initiation in Abydos? What drew you there?

This remote location in the Sahara, the Holy City of Abydos, is believed to be the oldest known place of spiritual pilgrimage—older than Mecca, Jerusalem, or any place in between.

From as long ago as pre-dynastic times, this location has been recognized as the absolute spiritual epicenter of Egypt and believed, by many, to be the spiritual core of ancient days, as far back as pre-dynastic record. There is the magnificent Osirion, which I now believe is truly the resting place of the head of Osiris (as intended to mean the thirteenth crystal skull). It is the primary passageway into the Halls of Amenti.

There are the burial grounds, soon to be excavated—these will make the current Valley of Kings look like a mere mini-museum.

There are the villages, magical unto themselves, where ancient temples lie buried here and there, in the sands of time. And, of course, there is the splendid Temple of Sety I of Abydos, the best preserved in the whole Egyptian realm. Here, the gods depicted in the walls and the energies they represent are alive—you can be transported and communicate with them. That, too, is part of a message I will soon share.

The temple of Abydos, a shrine built by the Pharaoh Sety I is the ultimate temple to the gods. It embodies the house of the Creator and mirrors the story of the struggle of darkness and light throughout time.

I was drawn to this temple because on many other occasions, during short visits on police escorted caravans, I have had just a glimpse into its beauty and just fleeting moments to experience its powerful energies. More importantly, I was guided by the Sirian High Council.

I believe that the Pharaoh Sety I still walks the halls and that his spirit is embodied in the temple, the grounds, and the holy city itself. In a way, I was drawn to follow the footsteps of Omm Sety, the extraordinary Dorothy Eady, whom you can read about in the work *The Search for Omm Sety,** to meet the past in the temple of Abydos and to ask the gods for guidance.

A woman with an incredible connection to this sacred place, she communicated with Sety I for all of her life, which for the most part, she spent in the sacred halls of Abydos.

---

*Cott, Jonathan, *The Search for Omm Sety,* (London: Arrow Books, 1989)

You said you would be aided and assisted by guardians and initiates. Can you give us more information about these people and how they are related to your work?

I have always been blessed with the support of facilitators in all the work I have done for Spirit. This has been accelerated since the first encounters with the Sirian High Council in the crop circle the Julia Set in 1996.

Inevitably and incredibly, everywhere events, people, and forces appear to me who are willing to unlock the locked gates, to open closed doors, and to share the secrets that are needed at that point of my journey—at that initiation.

In the case of Abydos, there are people who prefer to be unnamed so that they are protected, who have provided me access to secret spaces, underground tunnels, and sacred halls, where it is not permitted by the government and by the Egyptian authorities.

I believe that they appear in service, as I am, to help bring the information out as is needed now, part of their own spiritual process, and that this Family of Light is connected on many levels of consciousness. Whether fully aware of their role or not, they appear at the right time, the right place, and with the right intention—providing access to secret passageways for me and, in many cases, for those who travel with me. And I am grateful, so grateful to them, for their dedication, love, and assistance.

What do you mean about unlocking the forces of Giza? What does the plan about releasing these forces consist of?

The monuments at Giza and beyond the plateau, to include the lesser pyramids and the step pyramid of Sakkara, are all located above a gigantic energy plant with its underground city, which is, topographically, far more immense than the surface urban city of Cairo. There are extensive tunnel networks, roadways, and structures there and these are all related to the utilization of the Great Pyramid and its surrounding structures in the harnessing of cosmic energy.

We are becoming aware of the existence of multidimensional portals that lead through the dimensions, into other galaxies, other universes—and who knows where else. These portals are directly linked with the chakric centers and energy grids of Gaia herself.

Of these, the epicenter is Giza: the entire plateau is a gateway.

That is why the Sphinx was first created for us there.

That is why the great pyramids are there.

And that is why the Atlantean record keepers left their imprint below.

Following your work in Egypt, is there something that we, as conscious lightworkers, can do to help?

While you still can, visit these locations with the intention to raise the vibration, reveal the secrets, play the music, and activate the stargates. This is the task of all of us—as starseed—and it begins with the most humble sense of service to the greater good.

Required now is an overwhelming need for heart-centered consciousness and the conviction that, despite the illusions of darkness, we know we are a breath away from the great shift, whereby a new world unfolds.

The obstructions are increasing and it is becoming more difficult for so many people to release themselves from their fears and survival issues to truly dedicate to the bigger picture. This requires letting go of emotional issues and conditional love. It requires forgiveness and acceptance, and this too is asked of us now if we are to turn the wheels of Giza.

Be as clear as you can be of your own ego and how it wishes to distract you from the higher purpose, obscuring your focus, placing your personal experience and the manifestation of phenomena over the good of the entirety.

It is time to dedicate our thoughts to the ultimate outcome, the highest good of all life, as the overriding collective consciousness—believing, at the individual level, that this is not only possible ... it is our creation and it will most surely be our legacy.

The dissolution of the dark force is the natural outcome of our brilliant mind collective.

Will there be many portals opening in the years to come in Egypt?

Interestingly enough, the more the forces of opposition try to close us out of the sacred sites, the more easily we access them on other levels. Egypt holds many gateways and vortices that lead us to our memory of Atlantis—and to its validation. These secrets are being withheld because the powers that hold rank in this plane do not want history to be rewritten. They do not want the veil to come down, revealing all the secrets that they have withheld.

And so, on a physical sense, many discoveries in Egypt and in other sacred lands are coming to light—all is coming into the light of our evolving consciousness.

On other levels, as you intend to mean portals between dimensions or fields of consciousness, yes—absolutely. Egypt unquestionably holds many keys to our awakening. Below the Great Sphinx, Sirian effigy, lies the Atlantean Hall of Records. Below the Osirion is located the etheric Master Skull of the Skull Committee, which will be soon activated in Mayaland.

The stargates of Egypt, I believe, will open the gates of the entire world.

The questions in this book refer to the teachings of the Sirian High Council brought through in the trilogy: *The Sirian Revelations.*

The broad range of topics in the teachings includes:

Book One
The Cosmos of Soul: A Wake-Up Call
for Humanity

Let There Be Light
Emancipation
Conscious Clearing
Opening the Archives
The Geometry of Manifest Consciousness
Sacred Temples
Cloning and the Genetics Nightmare
Time and Eternity
Attunement
The One Coded Master
The Secret Government and the Space Conspiracy

About the Author

A native of the San Francisco Bay Area, PATRICIA CORI has been immersed in the New Age Movement since its inception there in the early 1970s. She has utilized her clairvoyant abilities in healing throughout her life, which has been dedicated in great part to the study of mysticism, philosophy, ancient civilizations, metaphysical healing, spirituality, and unexplained mysteries. In 1995, she founded the LightWorks Association of Rome (a non-profit organization), one of the first Spirit Centers to appear in the Eternal City. Its studios served as a healing center, school, and the city's only New Age Library. She is a prominent figure in the Spirit Movement, and is well-known on the international lecture circuit—actively offering courses, seminars, and workshops around the world, which reflect her broad knowledge of alternative methodology in healing and her remarkable gift of helping others rekindle and ignite the power within. She has been recognized and celebrated as a gifted shaman by indigenous spirit teachers of the Tibetan, Mayan, and Peruvian traditions. In 1996, she established the LightWorks travel club, SoulQuest™ Journeys, and that year led a group of spirit travelers, to whom she introduced the sacred temples and breathtaking spirit of Tibet and Nepal. She has since guided people through sacred sites in Asia, Mexico, Egypt, Europe, and Peru, awakening them to Earth energies and the Secret Wisdom. Patricia's books and CD, *The Sirian Revelations*, have enjoyed worldwide acclaim as a wake-up call for the expanding consciousness of humankind. They have been rereleased to a vast international audience this year by North Atlantic Books in conjunction with Random House Distribution Services, and are also available in several foreign language editions. She hosts the cutting edge web radio talk show, *Beyond The Matrix,* on www.bbsradio.com—a program dedicated to exploring new avenues of human thought and experience and the merging of science and spirit. Patricia has also made many radio appearances and has recently been featured in the documentary films *The Circle Chasers 2006, The Wake-Up Call—Anybody Listening?* and *2012—We're Already In It!*

DNA Activation Programs

Patricia Cori offers personal training in DNA activation and certification programs for DNA Facilitators, as directed by the healing teams of the Sirian High Council, in various locations around the world. These are:

Ascension Training Level One
DNA Activation

The process of awakening the light body begins with the healing and release of blocked emotions, thoughts manifesting as illness within the physical body, and the reintegration of the fragments of your being that have been left behind along your journey. As you cannot move forward without them, the opening segment of the course will be dedicated to calling them home to you—a most essential aspect of our preparation for ascension.

The two-day intensive course, facilitated by Sirian light beings, focuses on opening the energy byways, drawing from the multidimensional self the innate abilities that will accelerate your preparation for ascension. Guided by light beings from many dimensions, you will be shown the way to the acceleration of your spiritual and emotional experience—preparing the way for the activation of the third strand of DNA and the awakening of the light body.

Activation of the new crystalline matrix that is forming in your evolving being (the integration of the third strand of DNA) creates triangulation within the consciousness of every cell of your physical body—the trinity of divine awareness.

The entire energy body, the chakras and their corresponding glandular systems (particularly the pineal gland), the Ida and Pingala energy byways, the auric body—every aspect of existence in the world of matter is about to change and as one of the awakening, you are eager to accelerate that process.

Those of you who have come in to serve as guides and healers in the process of Gaia's evolution are called to Initiation: the activation of the third strand; chakric clearing; cellular regeneration; resonance with the higher frequencies; and connection with the galactic family of light beings.

This intensive training is intended (but not limited) to those who are ready to take the leap as the first of a two-part training. During Level II, DNA Facilitators' Program, participants will integrate the new energies, adjust to the newly attained frequencies, and develop specific techniques and procedures to assist others in healing the DNA and retrieving the fourth, fifth, and sixth strands, pineal gland activation, and strengthening their link with the higher beings who are serving in the process.

As we draw upon the patterns of all cosmic consciousness, we will also ground ourselves to Gaia, for this is our celestial home— as it will be for those who choose to ascend into the next dimension: the New Frontier. This, in absolute integrity, honesty, and conviction—for we are past the time when we can distract ourselves with imaginings, posturing, and spiritual rhetoric. We must clear away the distractions, prepared to walk in the light of Absolute Truth—at peace in our souls as we climb the spiral of return.

Ascension Training Level Two
DNA Facilitators' Program

At the inner level, Level Two participants build upon the ongoing process of anchoring the third strand, laying further ground for the assimilation of the second triangulation: the fourth, fifth, and sixth strands, with the opening of the Golden Heart and the accelerated pineal gland.

At the community level, where our focus is upon bringing the Light and Wisdom of the Overlighting Ones to the other, the course helps develop a more profound awareness and ability in the work of sound and its healing global and planetary properties, DNA healing, vibrational alteration of individual and environment, attunement to galactic grids, and the proper use of channeling for planetary and universal perspectives.

Students are guided as to the implementation of the service they have chosen to bring to the whole, at this crucial time of individual and planetary transmutation, and the work of serving as First Wave Ascension Team Members in their tribes and communities.

The workshop includes deep meditation work and group toning, guided by the Council, training and practice in DNA reading, and instruction for the practical matters of serving as a DNA Facilitator: cellular regeneration, the elemental energies, the properties of conscious water, star linking, and opening the channels of extra-dimensional communication.

For additional information about the exciting SoulQuest™ Journeys and DNA Activation and Facilitators' programs with Patricia Cori, please contact LightWorks Press or consult our website:
www.sirianrevelations.net

Index

2012, 48, 90, 99, 113, 157, 176, 177, 186

Abydos, 181–182, 187–189
Adam, 38
Africa, 8
Agharta, 117–130, 150, 159
Aghartan Leadership, the, 20
Akashic Record, 22, 139, 153, 154, 158, 175
Alexandrian Library, 152
Aliens, 14, 91, 95, 126, 160
All That Is, 17, 40, 142, 158
angelic beings, 20, 63, 161
Annunaki, 15, 23, 25, 26, 27, 38, 57, 59, 74, 88, 95, 103, 109, 110, 139
Anu, 58, 59
Arcturians, the, 30
Armageddon scenario, 99
Ascended Masters, 9, 20, 150
Atlanteans, the, 14, 15, 71, 109–111, 117, 118, 120, 121, 124, 126, 136, 139, 142, 146
Atlantis, 15, 20, 100–104, 108–110, 118, 120, 124, 127, 131–141, 144, 145, 149, 154, 167, 174–176, 184, 191

Atlantis Rising, 104, 118, 139, 141, 144, 169, 176
Avebury, 161
Ayers Rock, 161

chakras, 67, 109, 198
Christed One, the, 9, 81, 134
collective consciousness, 32, 33, 118, 127, 146, 179, 191
computers, 39, 94
cosmos of soul, xii, 5, 11, 13, 41, 72, 97, 131, 162, 167
Cosmos of Soul, The, 192
crop circles, 89, 170, 171, 196
crystal skulls, 133, 142, 144, 145, 176, 183, 184, 186, 187
crystalline matrix, 197
Cydonia, 26

Damascus, 161
Dark Priesthood, the, 15, 101, 110
death, 10, 15, 18, 38, 46, 49, 92, 100, 110, 122, 127, 138
DNA, xii, 21, 63, 64, 71–86, 93, 132, 145, 167, 184, 193, 194, 197–200
Dogon, the, 8